Nature's Treats
recipes for wellness

Coreenna Ong

Marshall Cavendish

This book is intended to provide educational information on the covered subject. All recommendations are made without guarantee on the part of the author or publisher. The recipes provided herein are not intended to cure, treat or prevent any diseases. They are also not intended to take the place of advice, diagnosis and/or treatment from a qualified physician or medical practitioner. Every individual is different and everyone reacts differently to ingredients, be it natural or synthetic. If you develop any negative reaction to any recipe, stop using it immediately and consult your physician.

Editor: Sylvy Soh
Designers: Bernard Go, Rachel Chen
Photographer: Joshua Tan, Elements By The Box

Published by Marshall Cavendish Editions
An imprint of Marshall Cavendish International
1 New Industrial Road, Singapore 536196

The author and publisher make no representation or warranties with respect to the contents of this book, and specifically disclaim any implied warranties or merchantability or fitness for any particular purpose, and shall in no events be liable for any loss of profit or any other commercial damage, including but not limited to special, incidental, consequential, or other damages.

Other Marshall Cavendish Offices:
Marshall Cavendish Ltd. 5th Floor, 32-38 Saffron Hill, London EC1N 8FH, UK • Marshall Cavendish Corporation. 99 White Plains Road, Tarrytown NY 10591-9001, USA • Marshall Cavendish International (Thailand) Co Ltd. 253 Asoke, 12th Flr, Sukhumvit 21 Road, Klongtoey Nua, Wattana, Bangkok 10110, Thailand • Marshall Cavendish (Malaysia) Sdn Bhd, Times Subang, Lot 46, Subang Hi-Tech Industrial Park, Batu Tiga, 40000 Shah Alam, Selangor Darul Ehsan, Malaysia

Marshall Cavendish is a trademark of Times Publishing Limited

National Library Board Singapore Cataloguing in Publication Data

Ong, Coreenna, 1975-
Nature's treats : recipes for wellness / Coreenna Ong. – Singapore: Marshall Cavendish Cuisine, 2008.
p. cm.
ISBN-13 : 978-981-261-423-0
ISBN-10 : 981-261-423-0

1. Cookery, Chinese. 2. Cookery (Herbs) 3. Herbal teas. 4. Herbs – Therapeutic use. 5. Beauty, Personal. I. Title.

TX724.5.C5
641.5951 -- dc22   OCN183180648

Printed in Singapore by KWF Printing Pte Ltd

Dedication

For my business partner Alvin, his wife, Mimi,
and my dear friend Joe. I'm enjoying our spiritual journey
together and I feel truly blessed to know you all in this lifetime.

Author's Note

As a child, I was smaller and skinnier than most children my age. However, I had boundless energy, was rarely tired and could seldom keep still for long. Thus, I earned the nickname "skinny monkey"!

Because of my size, many people thought that I had an eating problem, but this was far from true. I had a hearty appetite as a child, but was selective about what I ate. I didn't consume cold or soft drinks, rarely ate deep-fried, fatty foods and only indulged in junk foods like potato chips and instant noodles once in a long, long while. I wasn't deliberately trying to be finicky or health conscious; I just had a natural aversion to such foods, even now. My parents also played a significant role in my siblings' food preferences and mine; they often restricted our consumption of junk foods and soft drinks when we were young. Their trick was to fill us up with rice, soups, fruit, fish and vegetables during meals so we would hardly feel the urge to snack in between meals.

This preference for healthy food started early in my formative years. Mum was always brewing tonic soups for the family, while Dad prepared all kinds of wonderful, nutritious dishes that he would teach my mum to prepare. Fish, vegetables, herbs and spices formed a major part of my family's diet. We had a fairly traditional Chinese palate, so it only was much later in life, when I was about 12 years old, that we had our first taste of fast food; even then, it was out of curiosity.

Today, I'm grateful for my parents' tender loving care. As an adult, I'm fundamentally influenced by their values, to which I attribute my deep interest in herbology and food nutrition. Had it not been for their influence, I would probably not be pursuing a profession which I love with all my heart and soul, and this book would not have been written. So thank you, Mum and Dad!

Contents

Eating and Drinking for
Health and Beauty

Do you remember the last time you suffered a cut that healed quickly? That was a manifestation of your body's excellent ability to heal itself. However, your body needs to be internally conducive in order for its innate healing powers to be fully utilised. That is why it is so important to consume wholesome, nutritious foods and pure water.

You Are What You Eat

It is surprising that while most people in developed countries suffer no shortage of food, malnutrition continues to be a rising health problem. Studies reveal that this is due to an increased consumption of highly processed foods and beverages that are stripped of nutritional value and loaded with empty carbohydrates or fats. While such foods are filling and tasty, they may not have the necessary nutrients your body needs.

Before fast foods like burgers, fries, sodas and milkshakes became a worldwide phenomenon, health issues like obesity, diabetes and heart disease were relatively uncommon. These days, the rate of people falling prey to these illnesses is increasing at an alarming rate–a growth that corresponds with the global expansion of fast food chains.

Fast food is perfectly fine when consumed in moderation. It only becomes a problem it becomes a regular part of one's diet. Food should delight the palate while nourishing the body and mind.

Food As Medicine

There are many natural health remedies concocted from a variety of herbs, spices and common everyday ingredients. Some cultures do not even differentiate between food and medicine; they are regarded as one and the

same. Through ingenious combinations of various ingredients and appropriate methods of preparation, natural remedies are created to address a myriad of health, beauty, and psychological issues.

Chinese Herbs

Always buy Chinese herbs from reliable and reputable sources because dubious retailers and wholesalers are rampant in this trade, especially when it comes to expensive herbs like cordyceps, ginseng and birds' nest.

A few years ago, when I was shopping at a large herb wholesale market in China, I came across an impressive, seemingly established store that was selling cordyceps at less than a fraction of the normal wholesale rate. Naturally, I was tempted to purchase some, because the cordyceps looked really good.

Thankfully, I did not succumb to temptation that day. Soon after my visit to the market, the store was shut down and placed under investigation. Apparently, they were selling cordyceps adulterated with toxic chemicals that could lead to liver and brain damage. These toxins were used to increase the cordyceps' weight substantially to give unsuspecting buyers the illusion that they were getting a good bargain!

A friend of mine cautioned me against consuming Chinese herbs regularly. She claimed that whenever she took Chinese herbs, her blood test results revealed high mercury and lead levels in her liver.

Apparently, her friends had similar experiences too. On the contrary, I tend to believe that the problem does not lie with Chinese herbs per se, but rather the environment in which they are cultivated and processed. It is highly likely that land located near industrial zones or busy roads are contaminated to varying degrees, due to the presence of chemicals in the immediate environs. The air is also likely to be polluted with chemical fumes. It is little wonder that herbs grown in such areas tend to accumulate high amounts of toxic substances. Even in modern agricultural practices, harmful pesticides or herbicides are often used in herb and plant cultivation. It is therefore very important to purchase herbs from reputable trustworthy sources. Choose to purchase from organic suppliers whenever possible.

Getting Started

Many lament the lack of time, and being in a constant state of hurry and working on tight schedules, fast foods, instant noodles and other such foods have become diet staples. How healthy can that be?

If you are willing to break away from the mindset that cooking is time-consuming and tedious, and believe that it is possible to prepare healthy home-cooked meals and beverages with minimal time and fuss, then this book is for you. Most, if not all of the recipes in this book have been chosen due to their simplicity and ease of preparation.

One way to save time is to use a slow cooker. For dishes with gravies or soups and stews, simply put in your ingredients, add the appropriate amount of water and leave the food to cook overnight or during the day, while you are at work.

Hygiene In Food Preparation

This may be stating the obvious, but hygiene is a very important consideration to be applied at all times, be it for food storage, preparation or serving. The following set of tips serve as a checklist and guide.

General Tips For Hygiene

• Use the freshest ingredients you can find. Fresh ingredients are more likely to have their natural nutrients intact.

• When preparing soups or stews that involve raw meat, always scald the meat in boiling water before use, as scalding removes excess blood, fat and odours.

• Wash all fruit, vegetables and dried herbs before use.

• Clean and wash all cooking tools and apparatus thoroughly before and after use.

• Store all cooking tools and apparatus in a clean, dry place. Make sure they are completely dry before use, or before storing.

• Store dry ingredients in cool, dark places. Refrigerate if necessary.

• If possible, avoid handling ingredients with your bare hands. Use clean, dry utensils to handle them instead.

• Prepare just enough food for a day's consumption, if possible. Cover and store excess food or drink in the refrigerator, but do not store for more than 3 days.

Know Your Ingredients

Brief notes on some of the ingredients used are provided in some recipes. You may notice that some ingredients are used in more than one recipe for varying preparation. This is because most natural ingredients and herbs have a broad range of therapeutic uses; how they are used or combined will determine their role and effectiveness for that particular recipe. Hence, the notes provided will discuss the ingredients with the context of that particular recipe.

How To Measure Chinese Herbs

The unit measurement for Chinese herbs is *qian*. 1 *qian* is equivalent to the metric weight of 3.75 g.

Common Terms Used In Traditional Chinese Medicine

Qi

Literally translated from the Chinese word for air, *qi* is the vital life force that flows out of all living things. *Qi* is circulated throughout our bodies through our blood and via specific channels known as meridians. These meridians sometimes experience blockage, causing in a disruption of circulation of *qi*. This results in poor health, sicknesses or a constant tendency to fall prone to illnesses.

Yin and yang

According to Chinese philosophy, *yin* and *yang* are forces that are opposing yet complementary at the same time. The kidneys are viewed as the central source of a person's *yin* and *yang*, which is why many of the herbs employed in the recipes in this book have properties that nourish the kidneys. According to traditional Chinese principles, food is divided into *yin*, *yang* and neutral categories. *Yin* foods cool and moisten the body, while *yang* foods warm and promote the function of tissues and organs. Neutral foods are those that have a pH value of 7 or around 7. A balanced diet consists of sufficient components of these food categories. Our *qi* is at its best when our *yin* and *yang* are balanced, thus rendering good health.

Yin and yang deficiencies

A *yin* deficiency refers to a lack of nourishment that is required to cool and moisten the body system. Some signs of *yin* deficiencies consist of dryness in the throat and eyes, feverish sensations and flushed cheeks. *Yang* deficiencies occur when there is a lack of circulation in *yang qi*, or warming energy in the body. An aversion to cold, lethargy and poor digestion are some signs of a *yang* deficiency.

Stagnation

In traditional Chinese medicine principles, stagnation refers to a broad range of congestions that occur in various organs. Blood stagnation or blood stasis is retention or slowing of blood, which results in painful cramps that are commonly experienced by women during menstruation or after giving birth. Stagnation in the spleen leads to indigestion.

Dampness

This refers to an excessive amount of body fluids that lead to abdominal bloating, appetite loss, fatigue, sluggishness and stiff, sore joints.

Phlegm

Phlegm is a sticky, visible secretion that is expelled either through the nasal passages or by coughing. Its texture and colour serves as an indication of a *yin* or *yang* deficiency. "Hot" phlegm is thick and discoloured, whereas "cold" phlegm is thin and clear.

Detoxification

A healthy, body functioning at its optimum (a pH value of approximately 7.5) should have a mildly alkaline constitution.

Most people, however have what we call an acidic body constitution. This is due to an accumulation of acidic waste materials and toxins that are produced through an excessive consumption of foods like meats, refined carbohydrates, carbonated and caffeinated beverages, and other rich, oily and fattening foods. If these waste materials are not eliminated from the body on a regular basis, one might start to feel unwell. The symptoms include fatigue, sluggishness, weight gain, skin problems, chronic headaches and yeast infection. Although not life-threatening, not paying heed to these symptoms may lead to have severe health repercussions over time.

According to Professor Hatori Tasutaro, Head of Akajiuiji Blood Centre at Yokohama Hospital in Japan, acidification of the body can lead to an increased rate of ageing and to other long term problems like diabetes, cancer, heart diseases and kidney and liver failure.

So for the sake of good health and beauty, treat your body kindly and detoxify whenever necessary.

Green Bean, Coix Seed and Sweet Potato Porridge (*recipe page 26*)

Do You Need To Spring Clean Your Body?

How can you tell if your body is in need of a good cleanup? Answer this simple quiz to find out. If your answer is "yes" to more than three of these questions, a detoxification program may be just what your body needs.

1. Do you feel tired most of the time?
2. Do you experience headaches or migraine often?
3. Do you experience frequent bloatedness due to water retention?
4. Do you find it hard to lose weight?
5. Do you have dark circles or bags under your eyes?
6. Do you have skin problems like acne or rashes?
7. Do you often have a blocked or stuffy nose?
8. Do you experience joint pains or body aches?
9. Do you have strong body odour or chronic bad breath?
10. Do you constantly suffer from constipation or diarrhea?
11. Do you often feel nauseous?
12. Do you get irritated easily or have frequent mood swings?

Dos And Don'ts Of Detox

Detoxification is defined as the process of eliminating toxins, waste materials and other harmful substances from the body through external means such as consuming special foods and liquids, or through fasting, so that the body can achieve an equilibrium state of balance and harmony and function optimally. As opposed to following a rigid detoxification programme, I believe that eating a balanced diet, with proper servings of fruit and vegetables on a daily basis is all you really need to do in order to obtain overall good health. A balanced diet, with an appropriate intake of nutrients allows your body to cleanse itself optimally and safely everyday.

Do:

- Drink a cup of diluted apple cider vinegar 2–3 times daily to cleanse and nourish your body.

- Drink lots of water to aid the process of flushing out metabolic waste and toxins. Instead of cold water, choose to drink warm water, or water at room temperature.

Don't:

- Don't starve your body. Starving your body will only slow down its metabolism and consequently, its ability to cleanse and purify itself. Get your sustenance from brown rice, healthy, low fat soups, fruit, vegetables and other delicious natural foods.

- Don't overdo detoxification. Too much of anything is bad.

Additional Tips To Keep Your System Clean

- Drink a glass of warm water on an empty stomach every morning before breakfast. Add a teaspoon of lemon juice from green lemons, or apple cider vinegar to enhance the cleansing properties.

- Work up a sweat by exercising regularly and moderately to expel toxins from your body. However, avoid over-exercising as it may generate free radicals that age the body prematurely.

- Avoid consuming junk foods and chemically-processed foods.

- Practice deep breathing for at least 10 minutes every day in a well-ventilated area. You will be amazed at how such a simple technique can help you feel energised and refreshed almost instantaneously.

Aloe Vera Refresher

This refreshing dessert contains the cleansing and cooling properties of aloe vera. It is low in calories and is great for helping the body get rid of excess toxins. Aloe vera also happens to be a natural cure for indigestion or constipation. For those who dislike its bitter taste, this recipe will make eating fresh aloe vera a delight! *Serves 2*

Honey	to taste
Warm water	375 ml (12 fl oz / 1^1/$_2$ cups)
Lemon juice	4 Tbsp
Lime juice	4 Tbsp
Aloe vera leaf	1, medium to large

Method

1 Dissolve honey in warm water, then stir in lemon and lime juice and mix well. Refrigerate to chill.

2 Rinse leaf and slice off sharp edges and tough outer skin. Drain sap and rinse under running water to remove sap completely. Slice translucent flesh into 2.5-cm (1-in) cubes.

3 Add aloe vera cubes to drink. Serve chilled.

Detox Juice

Spring clean your body with this healthful concoction. *Serves 1*

Beetroot	^{1}/$_2$, peeled
Cucumber	1, peeled
Red apple	2, cored and seeded
Celery	3 stalks
Apple cider vinegar	1 tsp

Method

1 Cut ingredients into small pieces for easy processing. Place ingredients into a fruit juicer or blender, add vinegar and blend until smooth.

2 Serve immediately.

Nature's Tidbits

Beetroot
Contains antioxidants, carotenoids, flavenoids and detoxifies the liver, blood and kidneys.

Apple cider vinegar
Apple cider vinegar has antibacterial, antiviral, antifungal and antioxidant properties.

Aloe Vera Refresher

Body Cleansing Soup

This virtually fat-free soup is great for weight loss. *Serves 4–5*

Bitter gourd	1
Dried anchovies	70 g (2$^1/_2$ oz), rinsed and drained
Dried scallops	8, rinsed and drained
Celery	3 stalks, cut into 2.5-cm (1-in) pieces
Water	6–7 rice bowls
Salt (optional)	to taste
Ground white pepper (optional)	to taste

Method

1 Cut bitter gourd into halves. Scoop out the white pith and seeds, then cut into 2.5-cm (1-in) pieces.

2 Place in a pot and add anchovies, scallops, celery and water and bring to the boil over high heat. Reduce heat to low and leave to simmer for 1$^1/_2$ hours. Add salt and pepper to taste, if desired.

3 Dish out and serve immediately.

Nature's Tidbits

Bitter gourd
Dispels dampness and heat from the body, reduces blood pressure, eliminates toxins and relieves water retention.

Celery
Contains cleansing and diuretic properties, eliminates toxins and waste materials such as uric acid and has natural laxative effects. Celery juice is also an appetite suppressant and useful for those who wish to lose weight.

Honeysuckle, Dandelion and Chrysanthemum Tea

Honeysuckle, dandelion and chrysanthemum flowers make a simple but effective brew for clearing the body of toxins and excess heat. *Serves 1*

Dried honeysuckle flowers (*jin yin hua*)	3 *qian*
Dried dandelion flowers (*pu gong ying*)	3 *qian*
Dried chrysanthemum flowers (*ju hua*)	4 *qian*
Water	500 ml (16 fl oz / 2 cups)

Method

1 Rinse flowers and drain well. Place honeysuckle and dandelion flowers in an earthen pot, add water and leave mixture to soak for 20 minutes.

2 Bring mixture to the boil over high heat. Reduce heat to low and leave to simmer, covered, for 40 minutes. Remove from heat and add chrysanthemum flowers. Leave mixture to infuse for 20 minutes before straining tea. Discard flowers.

3 Serve warm or at room temperature.

Sour Plum Hawthorn Tea

Better known in its candied form, which is a favourite with children, hawthorn fruit is somewhat of a "multi-purpose" herb as it has many healing properties. *Serves 2–3*

Dried sour plums	10
Hawthorn fruit (*shan zha*)	3 *qian*
Water	1 litre (32 fl oz / 4 cups)
Honey or brown sugar	to taste

Method

1 Combine sour plums and hawthorn in an earthen pot. Add water and honey or brown sugar and bring to the boil over high heat. Reduce heat to low and leave to simmer, covered, for 30 minutes.

2 Remove from heat and leave mixture to infuse for 20 minutes before straining tea. Discard ingredients.

3 Serve warm or cool.

Nature's Tidbits

Hawthorn fruit (*shan zha*)

Promotes digestion, blood circulation and prevents stagnation of the blood and digestive system. Hawthorn fruit also reduces cholesterol levels and alleviates cardiovascular problems like hypertension and angina.

Honeysuckle, Dandelion and Chrysanthemum Tea

Thai Papaya Salad

Papaya is rich in papain, a powerful protein-digesting enzyme. This healthy salad helps to cleanse the large intestines and clear bloating and stagnation of the digestive system. Best eaten after a heavy, meaty meal. *Serves 3–4*

Papaya	1, small, peeled and cut into small pieces
Red cabbage	6 leaves, finely sliced
Cherry tomatoes	8, halved
Shallots	3, peeled and finely sliced

Dressing

Garlic	3 cloves, peeled and minced
Fish sauce	3–5 Tbsp
Fresh lemon juice	90 ml (3 fl oz / $^3/_8$ cup)
Brown sugar	to taste

Method

1 Combine all ingredients except dressing in a mixing bowl. Toss to mix well and set aside.

2 Prepare dressing. Combine all ingredients in a mixing bowl and stir to mix well.

3 Drizzle dressing over salad ingredients and toss to coat evenly. Transfer to a serving dish and serve immediately.

Note: Avoid consumption if suffering from gastritis or if you have an overly acidic stomach. People with acidic stomachs tend to experience bloatedness, pain and discomfort in the abdominal area whenever go without eating for prolonged periods or when they consume food that is sour and acidic.

Watercress Juice

Watercress is ideal for detoxification as it purifies, tones and cools the body. It also revitalizes the body by supplying it with important vitamins and minerals. *Serves 1*

Apple cider vinegar	3 Tbsp, mixed with 250 ml (8 fl oz / 1 cup) water
Watercress	100 g (3$^1/_2$ oz), rinsed and drained
Apples	2, cored, seeded and quartered

Method

1 Pour apple cider vinegar mixture into a glass mixing bowl, add watercress and apples and leave to steep for 10 minutes. Pour mixture into a fruit juicer or blender and blend until smooth.

2 Serve immediately.

Note: Avoid consumption during pregnancy.

Green Bean, Coix Seed and Sweet Potato Porridge

Due to its high fibre content, this dish is especially helpful for relieving constipation. Sweet potato is employed for its ability to moisten and lubricate the large intestines, thus easing bowel movements. *Serves 2–4*

Green beans	3 Tbsp
Coix seeds (*yi yi ren*)	3 Tbsp
Sweet potato	1, peeled and diced
Water	1.5 litres (48 fl oz / 6 cups)
Rock sugar or honey	to taste

Method

1 Rinse green beans and coix seeds and drain well. Place in an earthen pot, then add sweet potato and water and bring to the boil over high heat. Reduce heat to low and leave to simmer gently until ingredients are tender. Stir occasionally to prevent mixture from sticking to pot. Add rock sugar or honey to taste and stir to mix well.

2 Dish out and serve immediately.

Note: Sweet potato is an excellent natural laxative for women experiencing constipation during pregnancy. Omit coix seeds from recipe for consumption during pregnancy.

Anti-blemish Tea

In traditional Chinese medicine, it is said that excessive heat and stagnation in the blood causes an accumulation of dampness and toxins, all of which manifest on the skin as acne or boils. Drinking this tea regularly promotes drainage of pus and toxins, improves blood circulation and heals skin eruptions, sore throats and bloatedness. *Serves 1–2*

Fritillary bulb (*chuan bei mu*)	3 *qian*, crushed
Peach kernels (*tao ren*)	2 *qian*, crushed
Hawthorne fruit (*shan zha*)	2 *qian*
Lotus leaves (*he ye*)	2 *qian*
Water	500 ml (16 fl oz / 2 cups)

Method

1 Rinse herbs and drain well. Place in a small earthen pot, add water and leave to soak for 30 minutes.

2 Bring mixture to the boil over high heat, then reduce heat to low and leave to simmer, covered, for 40 minutes. Remove from heat and leave mixture aside to infuse for another 10 minutes. Stir mixture before straining tea. Discard ingredients.

3 Serve warm or at room temperature.

Note: Not suitable for people experiencing colds or blood deficiencies. Avoid consumption during pregnancy.

Nature's Tidbits

Fritillary bulb (*chuan bei mu*)
Useful for treating coughs and dissolving phlegm caused by excess heat in the body. Also useful for treating acne.

Peach kernels (*tao ren*)
Contains anti-parasitic properties, breaks up blood stasis and promotes blood circulation.

Hawthorn fruit (*shan zha*)
Eliminates excess fats in blood, promotes blood circulation and cures blood stagnation.

Lotus leaves (*he ye*)
Clears excess heat in the body.

Herbal Detox Tea

This herbal tea has moderate laxative qualities and should only be used as a short-term measure to cure constipation. Best taken once in the morning and evening. *Serves 2*

Immature sweet orange (*zhi shi*)	1 *qian*
Water	500 ml (16 fl oz / 2 cups)
Senna leaves (*fan xie ye*)	2 *qian*

Method

1 Rinse herbs and drain well. Place sweet orange in an earthen pot, add water and leave mixture to soak for 20 minutes.

2 Bring mixture to the boil over high heat, then reduce heat to low and leave to simmer for 30 minutes. Remove from heat and add senna leaves. Cover pot and leave mixture to infuse for 10 minutes before straining. Discard ingredients.

3 Serve warm or at room temperature.

Note: Avoid consumption during pregnancy when lactating and during menstruation. Not suitable for people with weak body constitutions, hemorrhoids or ulcers in the stomach and small intestines. Do not exceed recommended dosage as it can lead to nausea, stomachache, dizziness, numbness in the mouth and limbs, and swollen hands and fingers.

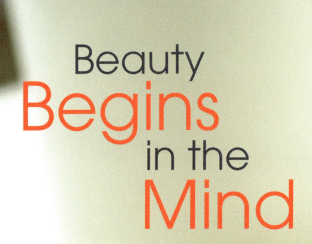

Beauty
Begins
in the
Mind

Surveys have shown that more people are turning to relaxants or anti-depressant drugs to help them cope with stress. The use and misuse of drugs, such as sleeping pills, are getting increasingly common among the working population, homemakers and even students.

Beauty begins in the mind. It is hard to feel beautiful when we are mentally exhausted, stressed, depressed or suffering from insomnia. To counter these problems and maintain a healthy state of mind, we should pamper ourselves once in a while. Besides the gamut of aromatherapy, massage and spa treatments available commercially, we should also look to good nutrition to keep ourselves looking fresh and feeling fabulous.

Spiced Hot Chocolate (*recipe page 32*)

Spiced Hot Chocolate

When Harry Potter, the protagonist in JK Rowling's book, *Harry Potter and the Prisoner of Azkaban*, regained consciousness from his fainting spell after encountering an evil creature known as a Dementor, his professor wisely made him eat a piece of chocolate. Almost instantly, he felt strength returning to his body and mind. The professor was right of course. It is wonderful to realise that chocolate is an excellent mood elevator as it contains phenyl ethylamine, and serotonin, anti-depressant ingredients that elevate one's mood. What's more, chocolate is packed with powerful antioxidants that are said to be beneficial to cardiovascular health. *Serves 1*

Cocoa powder	3 Tbsp
Ground cinnamon	$^1/_2$ tsp
Ground vanilla pod	$^1/_2$ tsp
Cold milk	85 ml ($2^1/_2$ fl oz / $^1/_3$ cup)
Water	170 ml (5 fl oz / $^2/_3$ cup)
Brown sugar (optional)	to taste

Method

1 Combine cocoa powder, cinnamon, vanilla pod and milk in a mixing bowl and mix well. Set aside.

2 In a saucepan, bring water to the boil over high heat. Reduce heat and stir in chocolate mixture. Stir to blend until smooth and free from lumps while keeping a gentle simmer.

3 Remove from heat and add sugar to taste, if desired.

4 Serve hot.

Note: Avoid buying artificially flavoured chocolate; always buy the purest chocolate you can find in order to enjoy its health benefits. Omit cinnnamon from recipe during pregnancy.

Nature's Tidbits

Vanilla
Like chocolate, vanilla is reputed to enhance one's amorous desires. It is also known to calm hysteria and lift a person's mood.

Soothing Herbal Infusion I

This tea helps one to sleep well by reducing irritability, restlessness and anxiety. *Serves 2*

Spirited poria (*fu shen*)	2 *qian*
Garnoderma (*lingzhi*)	3 *qian*
Water	625 ml (20 fl oz / 2^1/$_2$ cups)

Method

1 Rinse herbs and drain well. Place in an earthen pot, add water and leave mixture to soak for 30 minutes.
2 Bring mixture to the boil over high heat, then reduce heat to low and leave to simmer, covered, for 1 hour. Remove from heat and strain mixture. Discard herbs.
3 Serve warm or at room temperature.

Nature's Tidbits

Garnoderma (*lingzhi*)
Calms and stabilises the heart and mind while promoting a sense of well being and relaxation.

Spirited poria (*fu shen*)
Calms and relaxes the mind and reduces water retention.

Soothing Herbal Infusion II

This wonderful herbal tea has a fragrant aroma. Inhale its fragrance, sip leisurely and let it sooth your frazzled nerves. *Serves 2*

Dried rose buds	4
Dried lemon verbena	^{1}/$_2$ tsp
Dried chamomile flowers	^{1}/$_2$ tsp
Dried peppermint	^{1}/$_2$ tsp
Hot water for rinsing	
Water for boiling	500 ml (16 fl oz / 2 cups)
Honey (optional)	to taste

Method

1 Combine rose buds, lemon verbena, chamomile and peppermint in a tea strainer. Pour hot water over mixture to rinse. Transfer herbs to a teapot and set aside.
2 Bring water for boiling to a quick boil over high heat. Remove from heat and pour into teapot. Cover immediately and leave mixture to infuse for 10–15 minutes. Strain, discard herbs and add honey to taste, if desired.
3 Serve immediately.

Note: **Do not consume during pregnancy.**

Sleep Well Tea

Insomnia is usually a symptom of poor blood and energy circulation and a deficiency in the spleen and heart. This tea nourishes the spleen and heart, improves overall circulation and is best drunk at night before going to bed. *Serves 1*

Spiny date seed (*suan zao ren*)	1 *qian*
Salvia root (*dan shen*)	1 *qian*
Spirited poria (*fu shen*)	1 *qian*
Siberian milkwort root (*yuan zhi*)	1 *qian*
Licorice (*gan cao*)	$^1/_2$ *qian*
Water	500 ml (16 fl oz / 2 cups)

Method

1 Rinse herbs and drain well. Using a mortar and pestle, crush spiny date seeds lightly, then place in an earthen pot. Add remaining herbs and water and leave to soak for 30 minutes.

2 Bring mixture to the boil over high heat, then reduce heat to low and leave to simmer for 30–35 minutes. Remove from heat and strain mixture. Discard herbs.

3 Serve warm.

Note: Avoid consumption during pregnancy, when having diarrhea, or while experiencing a 'hot' body constitution with symptoms like hot phlegm, sore throat and fever. Consumption might also cause drowsiness, so avoid driving or operating heavy machinery.

Nature's Tidbits

Spiny date seed (*suan zao ren*)

Spiny date seed has excellent tranquilising and calming properties on the heart and mind. This herb is helpful for people experiencing insomnia, irritability and stress.

Siberian milkwort root (*yuan zhi*)

Siberian milkwort root is said to be useful in strengthening the mind and spirit, helping to stabilise the emotions and enhancing one's will power. It also helps a person relax.

Other Tips To Getting A Better Night's Sleep:

- **Don't go to bed on a full stomach. Allow at least 2 hours after a meal before going to bed.**

- **Avoid eating heavy meals or rich foods in the evening.**

- **There is a time and place for everything. Empty your mind of all thoughts and worries before you retire for the evening.**

- **Take a warm bath before bedtime.**

- **Avoid drinking coffee or caffeine-laden teas in the evening.**

Brain Power Booster Porridge

This delicious porridge is packed with nutrients like Omega-3 and Vitamin B complex, which are essential for optimal mental performance. These nutrients also help to keep the brain cells functioning healthily. *Serves 2*

Salmon fillet	1
Coarse salt	1 Tbsp
Dried anchovies	1 Tbsp, rinsed and drained
Dried scallops	5, rinsed and drained
Brown (unpolished) rice	125 g (4$^1/_2$ oz), washed
Water	500 ml (16 fl oz / 2 cups)
Canned sardines	1–2, chopped into small pieces
Flax seeds	1 Tbsp, crushed
Fresh parsley	1–2 sprigs

Marinade	
Light soy sauce	2 Tbsp
Ground black pepper	$^1/_2$ tsp
Ginger	2.5-cm (1-in) knob, peeled and minced

Method

1   Rub salmon with salt thoroughly and leave aside for 10 minutes. Rinse in water, then pat dry with paper towels before cutting into small pieces. Transfer salmon to a mixing bowl and set aside.

2   Prepare marinade. Combine all ingredients in a mixing bowl and mix well. Pour marinade over salmon and leave to steep for 20 minutes. Reserve marinade.

3   Transfer salmon and reserved marinade to a saucepan and add anchovies, scallops, rice and water. Bring mixture to the boil over high heat for 10 minutes, then reduce heat to low to bring mixture to a gentle simmer. Simmer for about 1$^1/_2$ hours, stirring occasionally.

4   Dish out into serving bowls, then top with sardines and flax seeds. Garnish with parsley and serve immediately.

For Fair, Youthful Skin

According to traditional Chinese healing principles, the skin is a corresponding organ to the lungs and large intestines. As such, when the lungs or large intestines become dry, congested or affected in any other way, the skin's barrier function, immune system and moisture level suffer as well. This could be the reason why many asthmatic people also suffer from eczema. This could also be the reason why many natural herbs and ingredients, such as birds' nest, dendrobium and snow pears, which nourish and moisten the lungs, have the same beneficial properties on the skin.

The ancient Chinese medical text *The Yellow Emperor's Classic of Internal Medicine* states that "energy is the commander of blood; when energy moves, blood follows." Think about it. The lungs are responsible for breathing, and the process of breathing produces energy, or *qi*. All living creatures require *qi* to live. Therefore, if healthy lung function encourages good blood circulation, the skin will benefit from this, as blood delivers digested nutrients to every part of our bodies, including the skin.

It is not too hard to achieve a healthy, glowing complexion. Eat right, and your skin will reap the benefits!

Imperial Everlasting Spring Tea (*recipe page 46*)

Anti-Pigmentation Decoction

A classic formula for lightening and preventing freckles and skin pigmentation by tonifying and balancing the liver, improving circulation and clearing up blood stagnation and blockages in the system. In this way, the skin's metabolism and regenerative functions are enhanced for progressive lightening of pigmentation. *Serves 1*

Salvia (*dan shen*)	4 *qian*
Albizzia bark (*he huan pi*)	4 *qian*
Red peony bark (*chi shao*)	3 *qian*
White peony bark (*bai shao*)	3 *qian*
Chinese angelica (*dang gui*)	3 *qian*
Dahurican angelica root (*bai zhi*)	3 *qian*
Peach kernel (*tao ren*)	2 *qian*
Uncooked rehmannia (*sheng di*)	2 *qian*
Bupleurum root (*chai hu*)	2 *qian*
Cnidium (*chuan xiong*)	2 *qian*
Peppermint (*bo he*)	2 *qian*
Water	375 ml (12 fl oz / 1^1/$_2$ cups)

Method

1 Rinse herbs and drain well. Using a mortar and pestle, crush peach kernels lightly and place in an earthen pot. Add remaining herbs and 250 ml (8 fl oz / 1 cup) water. Leave to soak for 30 minutes, then remove cnidium and set aside.

2 Bring to the boil over high heat, then reduce heat to low and leave to simmer for 15 minutes. Return cnidium to mixture and continue simmering for another 15 minutes. Remove from heat and strain mixture into a bowl. Return herbs to earthen pot and set strained liquid aside.

3 Add remaining water to herbs and return to the boil. Reduce heat and simmer for 30 minutes, then remove from heat. Strain mixture into the same bowl containing earlier strained liquid and discard herbs. Stir to mix well and divide into 2 portions.

4 Serve warm or at room temperature.

Note: Drink one portion in the late afternoon and a second at night before going to bed. This decoction should be taken daily for 15 days before or after, but not during one's monthly menstrual period. Avoid consumption during pregnancy or lactation.

Nature's Tidbits

Salvia (*dan shen*)
Promotes blood circulation, dispels stasis or blockages in the circulatory system and cools the blood at the same time. Often used in formulas designed to clear skin problems such as acne, bruises, boils and sores.

Red peony bark (*chi shao*)
Red peony bark has cooling and pain-relieving properties. It also clears excess body heat and blood clots and reduces swelling from sores and infections caused by heat toxins.

White peony bark (*bai shao*)
Treats gynaecological disorders such as irregular periods, uterine bleeding and painful menstrual cramps. It also helps to nourish the *yin* and balance liver energy in instances of excess *yang*.

Dahurican angelica root (*bai zhi*)
Helps to reduce inflammation and expel toxins.

Peach kernel (*tao ren*)
Contains anti-bacterial properties, helps removes blockages in the body and promotes circulation.

Skin Beautifying Soup I

There can't be a more delicious way to getting a healthy, glowing complexion than consuming this fragrant, tasty soup. *Serves 3–4*

Codonopsis (*dang shen*)	3 *qian*	Black jujube (*nan zao*)	2 *qian*
Solomon's seal (*yu zhu*)	2 *qian*	Ligusticum (*chuan xiong*)	2 *qian*
Astragalus (*huang qi*)	2 *qian*	Licorice (*gan cao*)	1 *qian*
Chinese angelica (*dang gui*)	2 *qian*	Lean pork ribs	500 g (1 lb 1½ oz)
Chinese wolfberries (*gou qi zi*)	2 *qian*	Coarse salt	2–3 Tbsp
		Salt	to taste

Method

1 Rinse herbs and drain well, then place in a small earthen pot and add enough water to cover herbs. Leave to soak for 40 minutes, then remove ligusticum and set aside. Reserve ligusticum.

2 Rub pork ribs with salt thoroughly. Bring a large pot of water to the boil and scald ribs for about 20 seconds each twice.

3 Place ribs in an earthen pot, add 1.5 litres (48 fl oz / 6 cups) water and bring to the boil over high heat. Skim off any fat or scum that rises to the surface, then add herb mixture and return to the boil. Reduce heat to low and leave mixture to simmer, covered, for 2 hours.

4 Add ligusticum in the last 20 minutes of simmering and allow mixture to simmer for another 20 minutes. Add salt to taste and stir to mix well.

5 Dish out and serve immediately.

Nature's Tidbits

Codonopsis (*dang shen*)
Codonopsis improves *qi*, nourishes blood and moistens the body.

Black jujube (*nan zao*)
Tonifies blood and the body's *qi*, and contains natural antioxidants that delay the ageing process.

Solomon's seal (*yu zhu*)
Nourishes the body's *yin* and boosts production of body fluids.

Skin Beautifying Soup II

This is another soup for a healthy, glowing complexion. *Serves 3–4*

Chinese wolfberries (*gou qi zi*)	3 *qian*
Chinese angelica (*dang gui*)	2 *qian*
White peony root (*bai shao*)	2 *qian*
Coix seeds (*yi y ren*)	2 *qian*
Chinese yam (*shan yao*)	2 *qian*
Dried longan (*yuan rou*)	2 *qian*
Licorice (*gan cao*)	1 *qian*
Whole chicken	1, cleaned, skinned and chopped
Salt	to taste

Method

1 Rinse herbs and drain well, then place in a small earthen pot and add enough water to cover herbs. Leave to soak for 40 minutes.

2 Place chicken in another earthen pot, add 1.5 litres (48 fl oz / 6 cups) water and bring to the boil over high heat. Skim off any fat or scum that rises to the surface, then add herb mixture and return to the boil. Reduce heat to low and leave to simmer for 2 hours. Add salt to taste.

3 Dish out and serve immediately.

Nature's Tidbits

Coix seeds (*yi yi ren*)
Smoothens skin, improves its texture and clears heat and toxins from the body, helping to maintain a clear, blemish-free complexion.

Chinese yam (*shan yao*)
Improves digestion, enhances metabolism and keeps skin moist and supple by replenishing fluids caused by dryness.

Dried longan (*yuan rou*)
Dried longan is great for fortifying the blood as it is high in iron content. It is especially good for women who are prone to anemia and its related symptoms such as fatigue, pale complexion and cold joints, feet and hands. Besides nourishing the blood, dried longan also enhances blood circulation and warms the body. Being associated with the heart, it has often been included in formulas used for treating insomnia, emotional stress, anxieties and heart palpitations.

Super Antioxidant Smoothie

Super Antioxidant Smoothie

Quick and easy to make, with no fuss at all, this smoothie makes a satisfying, healthy drink. *Serves 1*

Strawberries	125 g (4^1/$_2$ oz), washed and hulled
Blueberries	125 g (4^1/$_2$ oz), rinsed and drained
Fresh apple juice	4 Tbsp
Fresh orange juice	4 Tbsp
Plain, unsweetened yoghurt	125 ml (4 fl oz / ^{1}/$_2$ cup)

Method

1 Pat berries dry with paper towels.
2 Combine berries, fruit juices and yoghurt in a blender and blend on high speed until smooth.
3 Pour out and serve immediately.

Brown Rice Porridge with Dried Scallops

A nourishing recipe that may look bland, but is in fact flavourful and full of texture. *Serves 1–2*

Coix seeds (*yi yi ren*)	1 Tbsp, lightly crushed
Fox nuts (*qian shi*)	1 Tbsp
Chinese yam (*shan yao*)	3 *qian*
Red dates (*hong zao*)	4, pitted
Dried scallops	5
Water	1 litre (32 fl oz / 4 cups)
Brown (unpolished) rice	55 g (2 oz), washed
Salt	to taste

Method

1 Rinse herbs and drain well. Place in a mixing bowl and add scallops and 250 ml (8 fl oz / 1 cup) water. Leave to soak for 30 minutes.
2 Pour herb and scallop mixture into an earthen pot, then add rice and remaining water and bring to the boil over high heat. Reduce heat to medium and leave to cook, covered, for 1^1/$_2$ hours. Stir occasionally and add more water to adjust consistency, if necessary.
3 Add salt to taste and stir to mix well. Dish out and serve immediately.

Note: Omit coix seeds from recipe if consuming during pregnancy.

Imperial Everlasting Spring Tea

Enjoy this aromatic tea at leisure and reap the benefits of its skin-beautifying goodness. *Serves 2*

Solomon's seal (*yu zhu*)	1 *qian*
Dendrobium (*shi hu*)	1 *qian*
Ophiopogen (*mai men dong*)	1 *qian*
Adenophora (*nan sha shen*)	1 *qian*
Black jujube (*nan zao*)	1 *qian*
Water	1 litre (32 fl oz / 4 cups)

Method

1 Rinse herbs and drain well, then place in a small earthen pot and add 500 ml (16 fl oz / 2 cups) water. Leave to soak for 30 minutes.

2 Bring mixture to the boil over high heat, then reduce heat to low and leave to simmer, covered, for 30 minutes. Remove from heat and strain mixture into a teapot. Return herbs to earthen pot.

3 Add remaining water to herbs and return to the boil over high heat. Reduce heat to low and leave to simmer for 30 minutes. Remove from heat and leave mixture to infuse for another 10 minutes. Strain mixture into the same teapot containing earlier strained liquid and discard herbs. Stir to mix well.

4 Serve immediately.

Caution: Avoid consumption during pregnancy and lactation.

Nature's Tidbits

Adenophora (*nan sha shen*)
A cooling, *yin*-nourishing herb that moistens the lungs and encourages the generation of body fluids to prevent dryness.

Dendrobium (*shi hu*)
Keeps skin moist and well nourished.

Black and White Fungus Dessert

A cooling dessert that is enlivened with orange peel for added tang. *Serves 1–2*

White fungus (*bai mu er*)	15 g (¹/₂ oz)
Black fungus (*hei mu er*)	15 g (¹/₂ oz)
Coix seeds (*yi yi ren*)	2 *qian*
Red dates (*hong zao*)	6, pitted, rinsed and drained
Dried orange peel (*chen pi*)	1 *qian*
Water	750 ml (24 fl oz / 3 cups)
Rock sugar	2–3 pieces, or to taste

Method

1 Rinse fungi thoroughly to remove all dirt, then place in warm water to soak until softened. Trim off hard, gritty parts and rinse again thoroughly before slicing into smaller pieces.

2 Combine herbs in a mixing bowl and add 250 ml (8 fl oz / 1 cup) water. Leave mixture to soak for 30 minutes.

3 Place fungi and herb mixture in an earthen pot and add remaining water. Bring to the boil over high heat, then reduce heat to low and add rock sugar. Stir until sugar is completely dissolved. Leave mixture to simmer for 40 minutes, stirring occasionally to prevent burning.

4 Serve hot or chilled.

Nature's Tidbits

Black fungus (*hei mu er*)
Black fungus enhances one's complexion by improving blood circulation and nourishing the blood. Recent clinical studies have indicated promising results for black fungus in treating atherosclerosis, a disease that affects aterial blood vessels.

White fungus (*bai mu er*)
White fungus moistens and nourishes skin, and is excellent for enhancing one's complexion.

Snow Pear with American Ginseng Dessert

This highly refreshing dessert can be consumed either hot or cold. *Serves 1*

Ophiopogon (*mai men dong*)	5 pieces
American ginseng (*hua qi shen*)	1 *qian*
Licorice (*gan cao*)	$^1/_2$ *qian*
Chinese wolfberries (*gou qi zi*)	6
Red dates (*hong zao*)	6
Snow pear (*xue li*)	1, cored, seeded and halved
Water	435 ml (14 fl oz / 1$^3/_4$ cups)
Rock sugar	2–3 pieces, or to taste

Method

1 Rinse herbs and drain well. Using a mortar and pestle, crush ophiopogon lightly and place in the pot of a double boiler. Add remaining herbs, pear and water, then cover pot.

2 Bring mixture to the boil over high heat, then reduce heat to low and leave to simmer for 3 hours. Add rock sugar and stir to mix well.

3 Serve hot or chilled.

Nature's Tidbits

Snow pear (*xue li*)
Clear heat in the lungs and moistens the body.

American ginseng (*hua qi shen*)
Replenishes *qi* and *yin*, and helps to alleviate dryness by enhancing production of fluids.

Ophiopogon (*mai men dong*)
As a *yin*-nourishing herb, ophiopogon moistens the lungs and intestines, preventing dryness. It also calms and soothes irritability and restlessness.

Beautiful Breasts the Natural Way

In *Nature's Spa: DIY beauty treatments*, I mentioned that the main goal of breast care is not to increase cup size (although some women might enjoy this bonus), but to encourage women to optimize the health and beauty of their breasts through proper long-term care and nutrition.

Poor nutrition is one of the possible factors for under-developed breasts. Hence, good nutrition is very important for optimal breast development, especially during puberty. Many herbalists also believe that another "peak period" for healthy breast development is the postpartum confinement period, when the body's renewal and regenerative powers are in full gear.

However, if you are past puberty and not planning to get pregnant, fret not either. From personal experience, I know that a combination of proper nutrition and daily breast massages with the right blend of natural oils will go a long way in helping one achieve firmer, fuller breasts. Do bear in mind that results will not be immediate or achievable within a few short weeks, but invest patience and diligence in daily breast care and you will be rewarded!

Papaya Milkshake (*recipe page 57*)

Chicken Herbal Soup

This herbal soup nourishes both the *qi* and blood, creating a more conducive physical state for enhancing the breasts. *Serves 2–3*

Chinese angelica (*dang gui*)	4 *qian*
Red dates (*hong zao*)	10
Dried longans (*yuan rou*)	8
Prepared rehmannia (*shou di*)	3 *qian*
Licorice (*gan cao*)	1 *qian*
Black chicken	1, cleaned, excess fat trimmed and chopped
Chinese rice wine	3 Tbsp

Method

1 Rinse herbs and drain well. Place in a mixing bowl, add water and leave to soak for 30 minutes.

2 Place chicken, herb mixture and rice wine in an earthen pot. If necessary, add more water to cover chicken. Bring to the boil over high heat, then reduce heat to low, cover and simmer for 40 minutes, or until chicken is cooked and tender.

3 Dish out and serve immediately.

Note: Avoid consumption during pregnancy or while constipated, having flu, or a sore throat.

Pig trotters Soup with Peanuts and Papaya

Pig Trotters Soup with Peanuts and Papaya

A warming, nourishing soup that plenty of nutrients that can be easily digested by your body. *Serves 1*

Raw peanuts	200 g (7 oz), rinsed and drained
Water	2 litres (64 fl oz / 8 cups)
Coarse salt	2–3 Tbsp
Pig's front trotters	500 g (1 lb 1^1/$_2$ oz)
Unripe papaya	1, small, peeled, seeded and cut into small pieces
Red dates (*hong zao*)	12
Ginger	2.5-cm (1-in) knob, peeled and sliced into 6 slices
Salt	to taste

Method

1 Place peanuts in an earthen pot. Add water and bring to the boil over high heat. Reduce heat to low and leave to simmer for 1 hour.

2 Meanwhile, rub trotters thoroughly with salt. Bring a large pot of water for scalding to the boil and scald trotters for about 30 seconds. Remove, drain and rinse under running water.

3 Add trotters to earthen pot with peanuts, then increase heat and bring to the boil. Skim off any fat or scum that rises to the surface. Add papaya, red dates and ginger slices, then reduce heat, cover and leave to simmer for 1 hour. Add salt to taste and stir to mix well.

4 Dish out and serve immediately.

Papaya Milkshake

This delicious milkshake is full of proteins, vitamins and minerals essential for healthy breasts. The papain enzyme helps to break down proteins in milk and Chinese yam, enabling the nutrients to be more easily absorbed by the body. *Serves 1*

Ripe papaya	^{1}/$_2$, small, peeled and seeded
Fresh Chinese yam	45 g (1^1/$_2$ oz)
Milk	250 ml (8 fl oz / 1 cup)
Honey (optional)	1 tsp

Method

1 Cut papaya into small pieces.

2 Combine papaya, yam, milk and honey, if using, in a blender and blend until smooth.

3 Pour out into a serving glass and consume immediately.

Imperial Bust Tonic Tea

Composed of various herbs that serve to nourish and tonify the body, this tea helps women to maintain firmer, healthy breasts. *Serves 2-3*

Chinese dodder seeds (*tu si zi*)	$^1/_2$ *qian*
Vaccaria seeds (*wang bu liu xing*)	$^1/_2$ *qian*
Codonopsis (*dang shen*)	$^1/_2$ *qian*
Chinese wolfberries (*gou qi zi*)	$^1/_2$ *qian*
Chinese angelica (*dang gui*)	$^1/_2$ *qian*
Chinese yam (*shan yao*)	$^1/_2$ *qian*
Sichuan lovage rhizome (*chuan xiong*)	$^1/_2$ *qian*
Prepared rehmannia (*shou di*)	$^1/_2$ *qian*
Dandelion (*pu gong ying*)	$^1/_2$ *qian*
Dried tangerine peel (*chen pi*)	$^1/_2$ *qian*
Water	625 ml (20 fl oz / $2^1/_2$ cups)

Method

1 Rinse herbs and drain well. Place Chinese dodder and vaccaria seeds in a disposable tea pouch and seal securely, then place in an earthen pot. Add 300 ml (10 fl oz / $1^1/_4$ cups) water and remaining herbs.

2 Bring mixture to the boil over high heat, then reduce heat to low and simmer gently for 40 minutes. Strain mixture into a large bowl. Return herbs to earthen pot. Cover bowl with strained liquid and set aside.

3 Add remaining water to herbs and leave to soak for 10 minutes, then bring to the boil over high heat. Reduce heat and simmer for 45 minutes. Strain mixture into the same bowl containing earlier strained liquid and discard herbs. Stir to mix well.

4 Serve warm or at room temperature.

Note: Avoid consumption during pregnancy or while breastfeeding. Leftover tea can be stored in an airtight container and kept refrigerated for up to 2 days. When reheating, ensure that tea does not reach boiling point.

Nature's Tidbits

Codonopsis (*dang shen*)
Strengthens the spleen and stomach and enhances their functions while improving *qi* in the middle area, where the stomach, spleen, gallbladder and pancreas are located. Codonopsis also enhances the body's ability to digest and assimilate nutrients, tonifies its *yin* and promotes blood and fluid production.

Chinese angelica (*dang gui*)
An important herb particularly for women as it helps to tonify blood, promote circulation (hence, optimising the delivery of nutrients throughout the body) and relieves pain. It also clears blockages in the body, ensuring that all channels of the body receive nourishment and function smoothly.

Chinese yam (*shan yao*)
Chinese yam tonifies the *yin* and *qi* inherent in the stomach and spleen, and improves the ability of these organs to function.

Sichuan lovage rhizome (*chuan xiong*)
Sichuan lovage rhizome is used in many herbal formulas to treat irregular menstruation as it helps to regulate blood circulation and activate qi and tonify the blood while preventing stagnation in the stomach.

Prepared rehmannia (*shou di*)
Highly effective for nourishing the blood and correcting blood deficiencies such as anemia, which causes fatigue, weakness, pale complexion and dizziness.

Dandelion (*pu gong ying*)
Helps to clear heat and toxins, as well as lumps, soreness and abscesses in the breasts.

Herbal Soup with Pig's Stomach

The Chinese value pig's stomach for its ability to regulate and strengthen the stomach and intestines, and its digestive and assimilative capabilities. This recipe makes use of herbs that are known for their bust enhancing properties. *Serves 2*

Chinese yam (*shan yao*)	4 *qian*
Codonopsis (*dang shen*)	4 *qian*
Chinese wolfberries (*gou qi zi*)	2 Tbsp
Astragalus (*huang qi*)	4 *qian*
Pig's stomach	250 g (8 oz)
Coarse salt	
Corn flour (cornstarch)	
White vinegar	125 ml (4 fl oz / 1/2 cup)
Ginger	2.5-cm (1-in) knob, peeled and sliced into 6 slices

Method

1 Rinse herbs and drain well. Place in a mixing bowl, add 1 litre (32 fl oz / 4 cups) water and leave to soak for 30 minutes.

2 Rinse pig's stomach well and pat dry with paper towels. Rub with some salt and corn flour, then rinse again. Repeat 2–3 times in order to remove odour.

3 Bring a large pot of water to the boil and add white vinegar. Scald pig's stomach twice for about 20 seconds each time. Remove, drain and cut into strips.

4 Place pig's stomach in an earthen pot and add herb mixture, 1.5 litres (48 fl oz / 6 cups) water and ginger. Bring to the boil over high heat and skim off any fat or scum that rises to the surface. Reduce heat, cover and leave to simmer for 1 hour. Stir occasionally to prevent burning.

5 Dish out and serve immediately.

Note: Omit astragalus from recipe if consuming during pregnancy.

Chicken Feet Soup

As an ingredient, chicken feet may not appeal, but it has plenty of protein, and despite its gelatinous texture, no fat! It is an ideal food for women hoping to achieve fuller, firmer breasts without gaining unwanted weight in other areas. *Serves 3–4*

Chinese angelica (*dang gui*)	2 *qian*
Astragalus (*huang qi*)	2 *qian*
Water	2.5 litres (80 floz / 10 cups)
Vaccaria seeds (*wang bu liu xing*)	2 *qian*
Chicken feet	15
Coarse salt	
Ginger	5-cm (2-in) knob, peeled and finely sliced
Chinese rice wine	2 Tbsp
Salt	to taste

Method

1 Rinse herbs and drain well. Combine angelica and astragalus in a mixing bowl, add 750 ml (24 fl oz / 3 cups) water and leave to soak for 30 minutes.

2 Meanwhile, heat a frying pan over medium heat and dry-fry vaccaria seeds for about 10 minutes. Remove from heat and pound into a fine powder using a mortar and pestle. Set aside.

3 Rinse chicken feet, then pat dry with paper towels. Rub thoroughly with coarse salt and leave aside for 30 minutes. Rinse again and place in an earthen pot.

4 Add herb mixture, vaccaria seeds and remaining water to chicken feet. Bring to the boil over high heat, then reduce heat and add ginger and Chinese wine. Cover and leave to simmer for 2 hours. Stir occasionally to prevent burning.

5 Add salt to taste. Dish out and serve immediately.

Note: Avoid consumption during pregnancy as the herbs in this formula stimulate contraction of the uterus. Avoid going out into the sun directly after consuming as vaccaria seeds may increase the skin's sensitivity to sunlight.

Nature's Tidbits

Vaccaria seeds (*wang bu liu xing*)
Known for its abilities to remove blockages and promote blood circulation in the breast area. It is also used to treat gynecological problems associated with blood stasis, menstrual cramps and irregular or absent periods.

Stewed Beef with Herbs

Although iron can be found in vegetable sources such as spinach, molasses and lentils, nutritionists have discovered that the human body is better able to absorb iron from meat sources such as beef and liver. If you are not vegetarian or vegan, consuming small servings of red meat is still the best way to get your dose of iron. This dish supports healthy breast development by nourishing the blood, improving circulation and enhancing cell growth and repair. *Serves 1–2*

Lean beef flank	300 g (10$^1/_2$ oz), cut into 2.5-cm (1-in) cubes
Marinade	
Ginger	5-cm (2-in) knob, peeled and finely sliced
Garlic	2 cloves, peeled
Ground black pepper	$^1/_2$ tsp
Chinese rice wine	1 Tbsp
Dark soy sauce	1 Tbsp
Sugar	1 tsp
Corn flour (cornstarch)	1 Tbsp, mixed with 3 Tbsp water
Chinese angelica (*dang gui*)	3 *qian*, rinsed and drained
Chinese wolfberries (*gou qi zi*)	5 *qian*, rinsed and drained
Water	500 ml (16 fl oz / 2 cups)
Vegetable oil	1 tsp

Method

1 Prepare marinade. Using a mortar and pestle, pound ginger and garlic into a fine paste. Transfer to a mixing bowl, then add pepper, rice wine, dark soy sauce, sugar, vegetable oil and corn flour mixture. Mix well. Add beef cubes to steep in the marinade for 1 hour.

2 Meanwhile, combine angelica and wolfberries in a mixing bowl and add water. Leave mixture to soak for 30–40 minutes.

3 Heat oil in a wok until smoking hot. Add beef cubes and marinade and fry for 3–5 minutes. Add herb mixture, mix well and bring to the boil. Reduce heat to low, cover and simmer for 1 hour or until beef cubes are tender.

4 Dish out and serve immediately.

Note: Lamb can be substituted for beef. During pregnancy, omit Chinese angelica from the recipe.

Rolled Oats Porridge with Soy Milk and Flax Seeds

Start your day on the right note with this nourishing and high-energy breakfast. *Serves 1*

Water	125 ml (4 fl oz / $^1/_2$ cup)
Rolled oats	3–4 Tbsp
Flax seeds	1 Tbsp, crushed
Unsweetened soy milk	250 ml (8 fl oz / 1 cup)
Black strap molasses	1 Tbsp

Method

1 Combine water, rolled oats and flax seeds in a saucepan and bring to the boil over medium heat. Stir constantly for 3–5 minutes.

2 Reduce heat and add soy milk. Stir to mix well and simmer for 3–5 minutes. Remove from heat and stir in molasses.

3 Dish out and serve immediately.

Nature's Tibits

Flax seeds

Flax seeds are rich sources of lignans, a substance which is lauded to reduce the risk of breast cancer, prostate cancer and hair loss. Flax seeds are also found to possess estrogenic, anti-tumour and antioxidant properties, making them highly useful in the support of total breast health.

Rolled oats

Rolled oats contain protein, calcium and soluble fibre, which are essential for keeping breast tissue healthy.

Extra Tips for Vegetarians:

Increase your body's ability to absorb iron from vegetable sources by simultaneously consuming fruit and vegetables high in vitamin C on a daily basis. Avoid foods containing tannins and calcium, as they impede the absorption of iron. So whenever possible, do avoid drinking any kinds of tea, including herbal infusions, with your meals. As a general guideline, allow a time lapse of at least 1–2 hours between eating iron-rich foods and drinking your tea. The following foods are rich in iron:

Spinach

Raisins

Lentils

Tofu

Black strap molasses

Kidney beans

Oatmeal enriched with iron

Cereals enriched with iron

Nourishment for Fabulous Hair

According to traditional Chinese healing principles, hair health is governed by the state of the kidneys. In other words, strong kidneys begets healthy, lustrous hair. When our kidneys lose their vitality, due to ageing, stress or frequent ejaculation in men, problems such as premature graying of hair or hair loss can occur. Therefore, in order to achieve healthy, lustrous locks, we should nourish our kidneys and eat well!

Anti Hair-graying Tea (*recipe page 71*)

Optimising nutrition for strong, healthy hair and scalp

The following hair care tips are useful and easy to bear in mind as you go about in your daily life:

- Minimise your intake of salt and monosodium glutamate (MSG). Too much salt in one's diet tends to strain and overwork the kidneys. Have you noticed that hair loss and balding problems are prevalent in people who consume salt or MSG-laden foods such as potato chips, bacon, ham and sausages?

- Eat whole foods that are rich in nutrients like proteins, zinc, selenium, copper, biotin, vitamins A, B5, B12, and E, inositol, sulfur, iron, iodine, magnesium, and silica. Hair is composed mainly of a protein called keratin, and the lack of copper in one's diet is believed to be the cause of graying hair. Some foods that contain these nutrients are eggs, milk, nuts, whole grains, dark green leafy vegetables like spinach and kale, soy foods, seafood, beans, liver, red or yellow coloured vegetables like capsicum and tomatoes and fish.

- Massage your scalp daily to promote blood circulation.

- Brush your hair daily to get rid of dead skin cells on the scalp. Brushing also helps to distribute the natural oils produced by your hair follicles to the hair shaft, making your hair look fluffier and fresher.

- Avoid chemical hair treatments such as synthetic hair dyes. It is a well-known fact that such treatments damage the hair and may cause hair loss, scalp problems, hair brittleness or even premature graying in the long run.

Black Sesame and Walnut Dessert

A traditional and well-loved dessert that is packed with healthy goodness for the skin and hair. *Serves 3–4*

Uncooked white rice	30 g (1 oz)
Water	1 litre (32 fl oz / 4 cups)
Black sesame seeds	45 g (1¹/₂ oz)
Shelled walnuts	45 g (1¹/₂ oz)
Honey or brown sugar	to taste

Method

1 Combine rice and water in a saucepan and bring to the boil over high heat. Reduce heat to low and leave to simmer for 2 hours, or until rice grains are soft and mushy, like in a porridge. Stir constantly to prevent burning and add more water, if necessary. Remove from heat and set aside.

2 Heat a frying pan over medium heat and dry-fry black sesame seeds for 3–5 minutes, or until fragrant. Stir constantly to prevent burning. Remove from heat and set aside to cool completely.

3 Place black sesame seeds and walnuts in a blender and blend into a thick paste. Stir into rice mixture until well blended.

4 Return porridge to the stove and cook over low heat for 2 hours, stirring occasionally to prevent burning. Stir in honey or brown sugar to taste.

5 Dish out and serve immediately.

Note: Avoid consumption if having diarrhea, loose stools, or while experiencing an excessively 'hot' body constitution.

Nature's Tidbits

Black sesame
Prevents premature graying by tonifying the liver and blood.

Walnuts
Replenishes strength and energy in kidneys, prevents and corrects deficiencies such as premature graying of hair. Also an excellent tonic for the brain.

Anti Hair-graying Tea

The synergistic combination of herbs in this recipe helps to prevent graying. *Serves 2–3*

Fleece flower root (*he shou wu*)	2 *qian*
Glossy privet fruit (*nu zhen zi*)	2 *qian*
Eclipta (*han lian cao*)	2 *qian*
Mulberry fruit (*sang shen zi*)	2 *qian*
Water	750 ml (24 fl oz / 3 cups)
Honey (optional)	to taste

Method

1 Rinse herbs and drain well. Place in a small earthen pot, add water and leave to soak for 40 minutes.

2 Bring mixture to the boil, then reduce heat to low. Cover and leave to simmer for 45 minutes. Add honey to taste, if desired.

3 Serve immediately.

Note: Avoid consumption during pregnancy and lactation.

Nature's Tidbits

Glossy privet fruit (*nu zhen zi*)

A rejuvenating, anti-aging herb. Often used in combination with fleece flower root to prevent premature graying of hair through replenishing the kidney's *yin* energy and essence.

Eclipta (*han lian cao*)

Eclipta prevents premature graying of the hair by replenishing the *yin* energy and essence. of the kidney and liver.

Black Bean Soup

A delicious concoction that makes preventing hair loss seem too easy to believe! *Serves 4–5*

Black beans	300 g (10$\frac{1}{2}$ oz), rinsed and drained
Water	2.5 litres (80 fl oz / 10 cups)
Lean pork ribs	500 g (1 lb 1$\frac{1}{2}$ oz)
Coarse salt	1–2 Tbsp
Unseeded black jujubes (*nan zao*)	8 *qian*, rinsed and drained
Ginger	2.5-cm (1-in) knob, peeled and finely sliced
Salt	to taste

Method

1 Place black beans in a mixing bowl and add 500 ml (16 fl oz / 2 cups) water. Leave to soak for 1 hour.

2 Rinse ribs, then pat dry with paper towels. Rub thoroughly with coarse salt and set aside for 10 minutes. Rinse ribs again and set aside.

3 Bring a large pot of water to the boil and and scald ribs twice for about 20 seconds each time. Remove, drain and place in an earthen pot.

4 Add remaining water to ribs and bring mixture to the boil over high heat. Skim off any fat or scum that rises to the surface. Add black bean mixture and ginger and return to the boil. Reduce heat to low, cover and leave to simmer for 2–3 hours. Add salt to taste and stir to mix well.

5 Dish out and serve immediately.

Traditional Herbal Soup with He Shou Wu

The herbs in this soup work in synergy to promote healthy hair and prevent premature graying. *Serves 4–5*

Fleece flower root (*he shou wu*)	3 *qian*
Chinese wolfberries (*gou qi zi*)	3 *qian*
Black jujubes (*nan zao*)	3 *qian*
Chinese angelica (*dang gui*)	2 *qian*
Black chicken	1, large, cleaned, excess fat trimmed and chopped
Coarse salt	2–3 Tbsp
Water	2.5 litres (80 fl oz / 10 cups)
Salt	to taste

Method

1. Rinse herbs and drain well. Place in a small earthen pot, add 500 ml (16 fl oz / 2 cups) water. Leave mixture to soak for 30 minutes. Remove black jujube and pound until fine using a mortar and pestle. Return to herb mixture.

2. Rub chicken thoroughly with salt and rinse in water. Place in an earthen pot and add remaining water. Bring to the boil over high heat and skim off any fat or scum that rises to the surface. Add herb mixture and return to the boil. Reduce heat, cover and simmer for 2 hours, or until chicken is cooked and tender. Add salt to taste and stir to mix well.

3. Dish out and serve immediately.

Note: Omit Chinese angelica from recipe during pregnancy.

Nature's Tidbits

Fleece flower root (*he shou wu*)
Replenishes energy in the liver and kidneys. Do not use utensils made of iron or metal when cooking fleece flower root; use utensils made of non-reactive material instead.

Chinese wolfberry (*gou qi zi*)
Chinese wolfberry tonifies the liver and kidneys and is often used in formulas for treating hair loss.

Black jujube (*nan zao*)
Black jujube tonifies the spleen and the stomach, thus improving digestion. It is also useful for nourishing the blood and balancing emotions by calming the mind and reducing feelings of irritability.

For Your Eyes Only

The eyes are windows not just to our souls, but also to the health of our bodies. For example, liver problems manifest in the form of red, sore or yellowish eyes. In addition to internal body problems, some people also experience troubling eye diseases that threaten to rob them of their vision permanently.

Mr Soo Vee Keong, a friend of mine, is one person who can personally testify to the effectiveness of Chinese herbs in treating serious eye problems. Diagnosed with severe myopia since she was young, Vee Keong's sister, Rosemary, developed Choroidal Neovascularization, or CNV for short, in her left eye. CNV is a serious eye condition where new blood vessels develop underneath the retina. Treatment in the form of laser surgery left scars that resulted in blind spots in Rosemary's eye, and in November 2006 she was diagnosed with CNV in her right eye as well. Disillusioned with conventional medicine and treatments, Vee Keong resorted to administering Chinese herbs to his sister in the form of natural remedies and a special diet. In just four months, Rosemary's right eye showed a remarkable recovery. The prognosis indicated that she had regained about 98–99 per cent of her original vision!

In Rosemary's case, Chinese herbs were prescribed daily at a therapeutic level. The prescription was closely monitored and adapted according to her condition. The recipes in this chapter that follow only support general eye health, but they will help to nourish your liver and keep your eyes feeling fresh and looking bright!

Eye Energising Tea (*recipe page 83*)

Mother-of-Pearl Honey Drink

This drink helps to soothe red, swollen and painful eyes by clearing heat in the liver and balancing its energies. *Serves 1*

Mother-of-pearl (*zhen zhu mu*)	1 *qian*, rinsed and drained
Water	500 ml (16 fl oz / 2 cups)
Dried chrysanthemum flowers (*ju hua*)	4 *qian*
Honey	2–4 tsp

Method

1 Using a mortar and pestle, crush mother-of-pearl lightly. Transfer to a small earthen pot, add water and bring to the boil over high heat. Reduce heat to low and leave to simmer for 1 hour.

2 Add chrysanthemum flowers in last 10 minutes of simmering. Stir to mix well, then remove from heat and strain mixture.

3 Add honey to taste. Serve hot.

Nature's Tidbits

Mother-of-pearl (*zhen zhu mu*)

Relieves skin conditions such as eczema, reduces excess heat in the liver and neutralises acids in the body. It is traditionally used to treat painful peptic ulcers caused by excessive stomach acids.

Wolfberry Mulberry Tea

Brighten tired, fatigued eyes with this simple tea. *Serves 2–3*

Chinese wolfberries	
(*gou qi zi*)	5 *qian*
Dried mulberry leaves	
(*sang ye*)	2 *qian*
Water	375 ml (12 fl oz / 1^1/$_2$ cups)

Method

1 Rinse herbs and drain well. Place in a small earthen pot, add water and leave to soak for 30 minutes.

2 Bring mixture to the boil over high heat, then reduce heat to low and leave to simmer for 40 minutes. Strain mixture to remove mulberry leaves.

3 Serve warm.

Tip: For best results, eat the Chinese wolfberries while drinking the tea.

Nature's Tidbits

Chinese wolfberry (*gou qi zi*)

Contains a high amount of beta carotene, a nutrient essential for healthy vision. Helps to brighten eyes by nourishing the liver and kidney.

Dried mulberry leaves (*sang ye*)

Dried mulberry leaves are used to dispel excess heat in the body that causes fever, pain and inflammations. Thus it is employed in formulas created to treat eye disorders due to excess heat, which is manifested in the form of red, sore or swollen eyes.

Spinach Juice

Do not be put off by the vibrant green colour of this juice, as it is packed with vitamins and nutrients that will give your eyes a sparkling, healthy look. *Serves 1*

Spinach	375 g (12 oz), washed and drained
Ripe tomato	1, medium, washed and chopped into small pieces
Green capsicum (bell pepper)	$^1/_2$, washed, cored, seeded and chopped
Orange	1, medium, peeled and seeded
Distilled water	4 Tbsp
Cultured drink containing acidophilus	90 ml (3 fl oz / $^3/_8$ cup)

Method

1 Combine spinach, tomato, capsicum and orange in a fruit juicer and process to extract juice. Discard pulp.

2 Pour juice in a blender and add water and cultured drink. Blend until smooth.

3 Serve and consume immediately.

Tip: For best results, consume this juice and the Fruit and Veggie Juice (page 84) once daily. For extra nutrients, comsume with pulp.

Spinach Soup with Fish

A tasty, nutritious soup that is simple and easy to prepare. *Serves 1*

Salmon or mackerel	300 g (10$^1/_2$ oz), cleaned, deboned and rubbed with coarse salt
Dried anchovies	2 Tbsp
Water	750 ml (24 fl oz / 3 cups)
Spinach	500 g (1 lb 1$^1/_2$ oz), washed and drained

Method

1 Slice fish into small pieces.

2 Place in a pot and add anchovies and water and bring to the boil over high heat. Reduce heat to low and leave to simmer for 1 hour. Add spinach in the last 5 minutes of cooking.

3 Serve immediately.

Tip: Consume at least 4 times a week for best results.

Eye Energising Tea

Soothe and refresh tired eyes with this simple tea. For people who use computers at work, this tea is especially helpful for taking away the strain on the eyes from working on the computer for long hours. *Serves 2*

Cassia seeds (*jue ming zi*)	1 *qian*
Tribulus (*bai ji li*)	1 *qian*
Red peony bark (*chi shao*)	1 *qian*
Water	750 ml (24 fl oz / 3 cups)
Dried chrysanthemum flowers (*ju hua*)	8 *qian*

Method

1 Rinse herbs and drain well. Place cassia seeds and tribulus in a blender and blend into a coarse powder. Place in a disposable tea bag and secure tightly.

2 Place tea bag and red peony bark in a small earthen pot. Add water and leave to soak for 30 minutes. Bring to the boil over high heat, then reduce heat to low and simmer for 30 minutes.

3 Remove from heat and add chrysanthemum flowers. Cover and leave mixture to infuse for 15 minutes. Strain and discard tea bag, herbs and flowers.

4 Serve warm or cool.

Note: Avoid consumption during pregnancy and menstruation. People with 'cold' body constitutions or a weak digestive system, and those who are prone to anemia should not consume this tea.

Nature's Tidbits

Cassia seeds (*jue ming zi*)
This is useful for eye disorders such as redness, dryness, swelling, pain and irritation. It also clears heat and wind from the body.

Dried chrysanthemum flowers (*ju hua*)
This cools, soothes and moistens the body.

Tribulus (*bai ji li*)
Promotes circulation and clears obstructions in the body system. Tribulus also helps to brighten eyes, reduce itchiness, redness, swelling and fatigue of the eyes.

Red peony bark (*chi shao*)
Contains cooling and pain-relieving properties, with the ability to get rid of excess heat and blood clots. People experiencing redness, swelling and pain in the eyes as a result of excess heat in the liver will find relief by consuming red peony bark.

Fruit and Veggie Juice

This uncommon but delicious fruit juice blend refreshes your palate, especially after a heavy meal. *Serves 1*

Carrot	1, large, washed, peeled and chopped into small pieces
Ripe tomato	1, medium, washed and chopped into small pieces
Red apple	1, washed, cored, seeded and chopped into small pieces
Celery	2 stalks, washed and chopped into small pieces

Method

1 Combine all ingredients in a blender and purée. Strain and discard pulp.
2 Serve and consume immediately.

Keeping an eye on food

Research has shown that when taken together, lutein and beta carotene compete for absorption by the body. For optimal absorption of these nutrients, allow at least 2 hours in between consuming foods that contain lutein (such as blueberry and spinach) and foods that contain beta carotene (such as Chinese wolfberries, carrots and spirulina). For the body to absorb and make use of beta carotene properly, your liver must be in good condition which can be achieved by taking 1–2 milk thistle capsules daily.

Consider incorporating the following foods into your diet for long-term, good eye health.

Blueberries

Eat 125 g (4$\frac{1}{2}$ oz) fresh blueberries, or drink 250 ml (8 fl oz / 1 cup) blueberry juice daily.

Red wine

Drink 85 ml (2$\frac{1}{2}$ fl oz / $\frac{1}{3}$ cup) daily.

Watermelon

Eat 280 g (10 oz) watermelon or drink 300 ml (10 fl oz / 1$\frac{1}{4}$ cups) watermelon juice daily.

Menstrual Care

During menstruation, it is best not to consume herbs that build and nourish the blood, as they may inhibit menstrual flow and the process of expelling menstrual blood from the body. If menstrual blood is not fully discharged from the uterus, fibroids and other gynecological problems may occur later in life. However, women should consume herbal brews and tonics to replenish any nutrients that are lost once the monthly period is over.

To keep your feminine energy and essence strong, avoid certain foods that deplete the *qi* and *jing* (essence) from your body. And do not disregard the age-old advice of not drinking iced water or eating cold foods while having your period, as the consequences may be painful cramps.

Red Dates Longan Tea (*recipe page 97*)

Egg with Herbs

The following variations for this recipe are great for women have a cold body constitution and experience weakness, menstrual cramps and anemia due to menstrual blood loss. They are quick and easy to prepare. Consume only after your period has ended, twice a day, once in the morning and at night, for 10 consecutive days.

Egg with Chinese Angelica

Serves 1

Angelica (*dang gui*)	2–3 *qian*
Water	250 ml (8 fl oz / 1 cup)
Egg	1

Method

1 Rinse angelica and drain well. Place in a small heatproof serving bowl. Add water and leave to soak for 20 minutes.
2 Cover bowl with a small glass or ceramic plate and place in the middle of a small to medium-sized pot. Fill pot with water until it reaches two-thirds up the side of the bowl. Bring water to the boil over high heat, then reduce heat to low to bring to a gentle simmer. Leave to cook for 1 hour, then remove from heat and set aside.
3 Crack egg into a bowl and beat with a fork. Stir egg into angelica mixture until it starts to cook and curdle in the residual heat.
4 Serve immediately.

Egg with Red Dates, Chinese Angelica and Longan

Serves 1

Unseeded red dates (*hong zao*)	3 *qian*
Chinese angelica (*dang gui*)	2 *qian*
Dried longan (*yuan rou*)	2
Water	250 ml (8 fl oz / 1 cup)
Egg	1

Method

1 Rinse herbs and drain well. Place in a small earthen pot. Add water and leave mixture to soak for 30 minutes.
2 Bring herb mixture to the boil, then reduce heat to low and leave to simmer for 40 minutes. Remove from heat. Crack egg into a bowl and beat with a fork. Stir egg into herb mixture until it starts to cook and curdle in the residual heat.
3 Serve immediately.

Left: Egg with Red Dates, Chinese Angelica and Longan
Right: Egg with Chinese Angelica

Classic Nourishing Yin Tonic

This tonic is beneficial for women experiencing amenorrhea, which is abnormally low levels of menstrual flow. It is an excellent yin tonic that supports the yang at the same time, normalises the development of the female reproductive organs and promotes contraction of the uterus. This formula does not taste particularly pleasant, but as the Chinese saying goes, "Good medicine is bitter in taste." The ingredient, placenta may sound dubious, but it is in fact a very powerful yin tonic used in traditional Chinese medicine. *Serves 1*

Biota seeds (*bai zi ren*)	3 *qian*
Chinese angelica (*dang gui*)	3 *qian*
White peony bark (*bai shao*)	3 *qian*
Red peony bark (*chi shao*)	3 *qian*
Prepared rehmannia (*shou di*)	3 *qian*
Chinese yam (*shan yao*)	3 *qian*
Chinese dodder seeds (*tu si zi*)	3 *qian*
Broomrape (*rou cong rong*)	2 *qian*
Placenta (*zi he che*)	3 *qian*
Water	750 ml (24 fl oz / 3 cups)

Method

1 Rinse herbs, including placenta, and drain well. Using a mortar and pestle, crush biota seeds lightly. Transfer to an earthen pot and add remaining herbs and 375 ml (12 fl oz / 1^1/$_2$ cups) water. Leave to soak for 30 minutes.

2 Bring mixture to the boil, then reduce heat to low and leave to simmer for 30 minutes. Remove from heat and strain mixture into a large bowl. Return herbs and placenta to the pot and set strained liquid aside.

3 Add remaining water to pot and return to the boil. Reduce heat and simmer for 40 minutes, then remove from heat. Strain mixture into the same bowl containing earlier strained liquid and discard herbs and placenta. Stir to mix well and divide into 2 portions.

4 Serve warm.

Note: Drink one portion in the morning and the second at night before going to bed. If reheating, ensure the decoction does not boil. Avoid consumption during pregnancy.

Nature's Tidbits

Placenta (*zi he che*)

Placenta is a powerful tonic for replenishing *yin*, body essence and blood. It is widely used in instances where quick rejuvenation and age-defying benefits are required and is particularly helpful for women as it helps to balance and regulate the hormones.

Classic Decoction to Curb Excessive Menstrual Flow

This is a well known classic formula for women experiencing heavy, excessive menstrual flow and symptoms such as weakness, dizziness, lower back pain, irritability, reddish tongue, faint pulse, thirst, constipation, deep yellow urine and excessive discharge. *Serves 1*

Himalayan teasel root (*xu duan*)	3^1/$_2$ *qian*	Scutellaria (*huang qin*)	2 *qian*
Uncooked rehmannia (*sheng di*)	2^1/$_2$ *qian*	Phellodendron bark (*huang bai*)	2 *qian*
Prepared rehmannia (*shu di*)	2^1/$_2$ *qian*	Licorice (*gan cao*)	2 *qian*
Chinese yam (*shan yao*)	2^1/$_2$ *qian*	Water	625 ml (20 fl oz / 2^1/$_2$ cups)
White peony (*bai shao*)	2^1/$_2$ *qian*		

Method

1 Rinse herbs and drain well. Place in an earthen pot. Add 375 ml (12 fl oz / 1^1/$_2$ cups) water and leave to soak for 40 minutes.

2 Bring mixture to the boil over high heat, then reduce heat to low and leave to simmer for 30 minutes. Remove from heat and strain mixture into a large bowl. Return herbs to the pot and set strained liquid aside.

3 Add remaining water to herbs and return to the boil over high heat. Reduce heat to low and simmer for 30 minutes, then remove from heat. Strain mixture into the same bowl containing earlier strained liquid and discard herbs. Stir to mix well and divide into 2 portions.

4 Serve warm.

Note: Consume decoction twice a day, starting 2 days before menstruation begins and throughout the menstrual period. Women who are pregnant, or who have a weak spleen and stomach, 'cold' body constitutions and anemia should not consume this decoction. This tonic is for short-term use only.

Nature's Tidbits

Himalayan teasel root (*xu duan*)
Relieves pain in the lower body, arrests uterine bleeding and eliminates blood stagnation.

Uncooked rehmannia (*sheng di*)
Uncooked rehmannia differs from prepared rehmannia in its abilities. It cools blood temperature and clears excess heat, and is often used in herbal formulas to curb excess menstrual flow and nourish the body's *yin*, thus preventing dryness.

Prepared rehmannia (*shu di*)
Widely used for its ability to nourish the blood, tonify the liver and kidneys and treat problems like lower back pain and weakness, dizziness and faint pulse.

Scutellaria (*huang qin*)
Cools blood temperature, stops excessive bleeding and eliminates dampness and toxins.

Phellodendron bark (*huang bai*)
Clears damp heat in the body, which causes problems like leucorrhea. Reduces excessive dry heat and eliminates toxins from the body.

PMS Relief Tea

This warming tea helps to relieve pre-menstrual abdominal pain caused by stagnant blood and *qi*. *Serves 1*

Lychee seed (*li zhi he*)	3 *qian*
Cyperus (*xiang fu*)	3 *qian*
Water	500 ml (16 fl oz / 2 cups)

Method

1 Rinse herbs and drain well. Place in an earthen pot, add water and leave to soak for 30 minutes.

2 Bring mixture to the boil, then reduce heat and leave to simmer for 40 minutes. Remove from heat and set aside. Leave mixture to infuse for another 10 minutes, then strain and discard herbs.

3 Serve warm.

Note: Consume tea twice day for approximately 5 days before menstruation begins. Avoid consumption if experiencing excessive body heat or if having a '*yin*' deficiency.

Nature's Tidbits

Lychee seed (*li zhi he*)

A "warming" herb that disperses cold and activates *qi* flow. Useful for relieving pain caused by blood stagnation and cold.

Cyperus (*xiang fu*)

Regulates *qi* in the blood and liver, enhances blood production and disperses liver stagnation. Also useful for relieving pain and cramps.

Herbal Lamb Soup

This nutritious, tasty and warming soup will provide you some welcome relief during your menstrual period, especially when experiencing cramps. *Serves 1*

Chinese angelica (*dang gui*)	4 *qian*
Red dates (*hong zao*)	6 *qian*
Poria (*fu ling*)	2 *qian*
Licorice (*gan cao*)	1 *qian*
Ligusticum (*chuan xiong*)	3 *qian*
Lean cut of lamb	500 g (1 lb 1¹/₂ oz), cut into small pieces
Ginger	2.5-cm (1-in) knob, peeled, sliced and crushed
Salt	to taste

Method

1 Rinse herbs and drain well. Place in an earthen pot and add enough water to cover herbs. Leave mixture to soak for 30 minutes, then remove ligusticum and set aside.

2 Bring a large pot of water to the boil and scald lamb twice for about 30 seconds each time. Drain and place lamb in a mixing bowl. Add ginger and mix well. Cover and leave to marinate for 1 hour.

3 Transfer lamb and ginger to an earthen pot, add 1.75 litres (59 fl oz / 7²/₅ cups) water and bring to the boil over high heat. Skim off any fat or scum that rises to the surface. Pour in herb mixture and return to the boil. Reduce heat to low and leave to simmer for 2 hours.

4 Add ligusticum in the last 30 minutes of simmering. Add salt to taste.

5 Dish out and serve immediately.

Note: Avoid consumption during pregnancy. However, women who have just given birth may consume this dish as it has restorative powers for the body, and promotes healing.

Red Date Longan Tea

This delicious tea calms and soothes frazzled nerves, enhances *qi* and blood production, and is especially good for you if you are anemic or experiencing chronic cold hands and feet. *Serves 4–5*

Unseeded red dates
  (*hong zao*)   30
Dried longans
  (*yuan rou*)   20
Dried tangerine peel
  (*chen pi*)   3

Method

1 Rinse ingredients and drain well. Place in an earthen pot, add 250 ml (8 fl oz / 1 cup) water and leave to soak for 30 minutes.

2 Bring mixture to the boil over high heat, then reduce heat to low and leave to simmer for 40 minutes.

3 Serve hot.

Note: Avoid consumption if you are experiencing excessive body heat, indigestion, constipation or when having a cold.

Other Ways to Relieve Cramps:

• Keep your lower body warm. If you live in a cold country or stay in an air-conditioned environment most of the time, make sure you wear warm and comfortable pants, skirts or leggings.

• Soak just the lower half of your body in warm water (water temperature should range between 38°C and 40°C) to relax the muscles in the lower region of the body. This will also help to relax the uterus.

• Do not lift or carry heavy objects.

Rose Tincture

Rose tincture is useful for treating fatigue, tension, stress, irregular menstrual periods, PMS and indigestion. It also helps lift the spirit when feeling depressed. A tincture is a convenient way to extract the maximum therapeutic effects from a herb. Several types of menstruum, or liquid used for extracting the active constituents of herbs and plants, can be used for preparing tinctures, but alcohol is the most common, and has good keeping properties. This recipe uses dried rosebuds, but try using fresh rose petals of the rosa rugosa or rosa gallica variety, if available. *Makes 250 ml (8 fl oz / 1 cup)*

Vodka (80–90% proof)	125 ml (4 fl oz / $^1/_2$ cup)
Dried rosebuds	55 g (2 oz)
Water	250 ml (8 fl oz) / 1 cup, warm or at room temperature

Method

1 Rinse rosebuds and drain well, then place in a clean, dry jar with an airtight seal. Add vodka and seal jar securely.

2 Store in a warm dark place away from sunlight. Leave to soak for 2–3 weeks and shake jar gently on a daily basis, to encourage the extraction process.

3 Strain mixture into an airtight container and discard rosebuds.

4 Mix 1 tsp tincture with water and drink immediately. Store remaining tincture in a cool, dark place.

Note: Drink a portion of tincture as directed above 2–3 times daily. Avoid consumption during pregnancy and breastfeeding. Tinctures can keep up to 2 years if stored unopened in a cool, dark place. Use within 6 months of opening for optimal potency and freshness.

Beautiful
Mums

Congratulations! You have entered one of the most significant phases of a woman's life. Having conceived a child, your body will undergo tremendous change as it taps into the creative powers of nature to make sure that the new life growing inside you is well supplied with all that it needs to develop a beautiful baby.

That also means you need to take extra care to keep you and your baby healthy, as you go through this remarkable period of life. Try these recipes and I guarantee you will have the vitality to embrace motherhood in a dynamic, glowing way!

Ginger and Lemon Grass Tea (*recipe page 110*)

Basic Dietary Guidelines During Pregnancy

Do:

• Maintain a healthy, nutritious diet packed with proteins, vitamins and minerals.

• Consume thoroughly cooked, easily digestable foods and soups.

• Minimise intake of salt and greasy foods to prevent edema.

• Eat regularly and sufficiently without overeating.

Don't:

• Don't consume cold, raw processed foods (with the exception of fruit and vegetables) and cold beverages and ice cream.

• Don't consume hot, spicy foods, at least during the first trimester of your pregnancy. Small quantities of such foods may be consumed sparingly as your pregnancy progresses.

• Don't drink alcohol.

• Don't smoke, or go to places where you will be exposed to smoke.

Preventing And Minimising Stretch Marks

Stretch marks are a common concern amongst pregnant women. As the saying goes, prevention is better than cure. If you keep your skin and health in tip-top condition, your body has a greater propensity to heal and regenerate. While there is no surefire way to prevent stretch marks, much can still be done to minimise their appearance through proper nutrition and skincare.

Minimise Your Sugar Intake

Studies have shown that stretch marks have a direct relation to the body's sugar levels. Minimising your sugar intake may help to prevent them from occuring. This is because the excess sugars bind themselves to protein, which makes up our skin's collagen and elastin. When this happens, collagen and elastin structures become brittle over time and lose their elasticity. The loss of elasticity also means that skin will sag and lose its firmness.

Get Your Dose Of Proanthanols And OPCs

Increase your dietary intake of foods rich in proanthanols or OPCs (Oligomeric Procyanthocyanidins) such as blueberries, strawberries and grape seed extract supplements. Please refer to page 45 for a proanthanol-rich recipe.

Moisturise!

Keep your skin well moisturised. Massage a small amount of natural plant oil onto your tummy, buttock and thigh area after your daily shower. Most natural plant oils are rich in essentail fatty acids which keep your skin strong and healthy. An Anti-Stretch Mark Oil recipe is provided in my other book, Nature's Spa: DIY Beauty Treatments.

Avoid An Excessive Dose Of Iron

Do not overly consume iron-rich foods as doing so may cause constipation.

Take Your Proteins

Elastin is a flexible protein structure. Therefore, keep up with your dietary requirements of protein throughout pregnancy so that your cells have sufficient nourishment to constantly renew and regenerate. Foods rich in natural glycoasaminoglycans and gelatinous substances, such as fish maw, sea cucumbers and pork trotters will not hurt either.

Miscarriages And Abortions

The aftermath of a miscarriage or abortion can be devastating to the woman and possibly, to her partner too. Besides emotional pain, a woman's physical health may also be affected.

If such an unfortunate event takes place, it is essential that a woman take extra good care of herself, just as she would after giving birth. Eat plenty of nourishing foods and avoid cold foods and beverages. Take time out to rest and relax sufficiently to allow total healing of the mind and body.

Morning Sickness Relief Tea

Curb nausea through this classic remedy for treating morning sickness! *Serves 1*

Ginger	1-cm ($^1/_2$-in) knob, peeled and finely sliced
Brown sugar	1 tsp
Freshly boiled water	250 ml (8 fl oz / 1 cup)

Method

1 Using a mortar and pestle, crush ginger slices. Place in a mug and add sugar.

2 Add water and stir to dissolve sugar completely. Cover and leave to infuse for 20 minutes.

3 Serve warm.

Rose Tea

Rose petals and rosebuds can help rid the body of toxins, improve digestion and clear blood clots. Rose tea makes for a soothing cuppa and is perfect for relieving headaches, calming and strengthening the nerves, and soothing post-natal blues. *Serves 1*

Dried rose petals or fresh rosebuds	1 tsp ,rinsed and drained
Water	250 ml (8 fl oz / 1 cup)
Honey (optional)	to taste

Method

1 Place rose petals or rosebuds in a small teapot. Bring water to the boil and pour over rose petals or rosebuds. Cover and leave to infuse for 15 minutes. Strain mixture and discard rose petals or rosebuds. Add honey to taste, if desired. Stir to mix well.

2 Serve hot.

Note: Avoid consumption during pregnancy.

Carp and Adzuki Bean Soup

Carp is not only nourishing for the body but it also helps to improve digestion and milk secretion for the nursing mother. It has good diuretic properties and is also useful for calming restlessness and irritability during pregnancy. *Serves 4–5*

Carp	500 g (1 lb 1½ oz), cleaned, gutted and deboned
Coarse salt	2–3 Tbsp
Adzuki beans (*chi xiao dou*)	150 g ($5^1/_3$ oz), rinsed and drained
Ginger	2.5-cm (1-in) knob, peeled and sliced into 5 slices
Black vinegar	2 Tbsp
Water	2.5 litres (80 fl oz / 10 cups)
Salt	to taste

Method

1 Rub carp with salt thoroughly and set aside for 5 minutes. Rinse under a running tap and pat dry with paper towels. Cut into 2.5-cm (1-in) pieces and place in an earthen pot.

2 Add adzuki beans, ginger, vinegar and water. Bring to the boil over high heat, then reduce heat and simmer for 2 hours. Add salt to taste. Stir to mix well.

3 Dish out and serve immediately.

Nature's Tidbits

Adzuki beans

Regulates water circulation and prevents edema. Adzuki beans are also good for clearing toxins and damp heat from the body, enhancing milk production while breastfeeding.

Pork Ribs with Apple Soup

This warming and nutritious soup is safe for pregnant women to consume even on a daily basis. *Serves 6–8*

Codonopsis root (*dang shen*)	4 *qian*
Poria (*fu ling*)	3 *qian*
Solomon's seal (*yu zhu*)	3 *qian*
Black dates (*nan zhao*)	10, seeded
Water	3 litres (96 fl oz / 12 cups)
Lean pork ribs	500 g (1 lb 1 1/2 oz)
Coarse salt	2–3 Tbsp
Red apple	1, cored, seeded and quartered
Ginger	2.5-cm (1-in) knob, peeled and sliced
Salt to taste	

Method

1 Rinse herbs and drain well. Place in a bowl, add 500 ml (16 fl oz / 2 cups) water and leave to soak for 30 minutes.

2 Rub pork with salt thoroughly. Bring a large pot of water for scalding to the boil and scald ribs twice for about 20 seconds each time.

3 Place pork in an earthen pot, add remaining water and bring to the boil over high heat. Skim off any fat or scum that rises to the surface. Pour in herb mixture, add apple and ginger and return to the boil. Reduce heat and simmer mixture for 2 hours. Add salt to taste and stir to mix well.

4 Dish out and serve immediately.

Beef and Carrot Soup

A hearty, tasty soup that is rich in iron, protein and vitamins. *Serves 3–4*

Lean beef ribs	500 g (1 lb 1^1/$_2$ oz)
Coarse salt	2–3 Tbsp
Water	2.5 litres (80 fl oz / 10 cups)
Carrot	1, peeled and chopped
Celery	150 g (5^1/$_3$ oz), chopped
Cooking oil	1 Tbsp
Onion	1, large, peeled and finely sliced
Tomato	1, large, finely diced
Salt	to taste

Method

1 Rub beef with salt thoroughly, then rinse under a running tap. Bring a large pot of water to the boil and scald ribs for about 30 seconds.

2 Place ribs in a pot and add water. Bring to the boil over high heat and skim off any fat or scum that rises to the surface. Add carrot and celery, reduce heat to low and leave to simmer until ingredients are tender.

3 Meanwhile, heat oil in a frying pan over medium heat. Fry onions for 3–5 minutes, or until fragrant, then remove from heat and add to the pot. Add tomato and leave soup to simmer for 1^1/$_2$ hours. Add salt to taste and stir to mix well.

4 Dish out and serve immediately.

Sour Plum Tea

This tea is great for dispelling nausea. At the same time, it quenches thirst and improve one's appetite. Drink small amounts of tea throughout the day whenever you are thirsty or nauseous. *Serves 6–8*

Dried sour plums	8, large
Freshly boiled water	1.5 litres (48 fl oz / 6 cups)

Method

1 Place sour plums in a large teapot. Add water, cover and leave to steep for 40 minutes, or until sour plums have softened.

2 Remove sour plums from teapot and scrape as much flesh off as possible. Discard seeds. Return flesh to teapot and stir to mix well. Leave to steep for another 10 minutes.

3 Serve warm.

Beef and Carrot Soup

Red Rice Porridge with Ginger, Anchovies and Red Dates

This delicious high-fibre dish will help to ease constipation that some women experience during preganany. *Serves 1*

Dried anchovies	2 Tbsp
Dried scallops	2, rinsed and drained
Unseeded red dates (*hong zao*)	6 pieces, halved
Red unpolished rice	55 g (2 oz), washed and drained
Ginger	1-cm ($^1/_2$-in) knob, peeled and finely sliced
Water	375 ml (12 fl oz / $1^1/_2$ oz)
Salt	to taste

Method

1 Rinse anchovies, scallops and red dates. Drain well and place in a small earthen pot. Add rice, ginger and water and bring to the boil over high heat.

2 Reduce heat to low and leave to simmer for $1^1/_2$ hours. Stir occasionally to prevent burning and add more water, if necessary. Add salt to taste and stir to mix well.

3 Dish out and serve immediately.

Ginger and Lemon Grass Tea

This warming and stimulating concoction is useful for dispelling wind and coldness from the body. *Serves 4–5*

Ginger	55 g (2 oz), peeled and sliced
Lemon grass	1 stalk, tough outer leaves removed, bruised and chopped
Water	750 ml (24 fl oz / 3 cups)
Dark brown sugar	3–5 tsp

Method

1 Using a mortar and pestle, crush ginger and lemon grass lightly. Place in a small earthen pot and add water.

2 Bring mixture to the boil over high heat, then reduce heat to low and add sugar. Leave mixture to simmer for $1–1^1/_2$ hours, then remove from heat and strain. Discard ginger and lemon grass.

3 Serve warm.

Oat and Bran Meal Porridge with Soy Milk

It is a Chinese belief that if a pregnant woman drinks soy milk daily, her baby will be blessed with fair, beautiful and healthy skin for life. While there is no scientific evidence to prove this, my younger sister is a real-life testimony—my mother drank soy milk daily while expecting her. How I wish my mother had done the same when she was expecting me! *Serves 1*

Rolled oats	2 Tbsp
Bran meal	1 Tbsp
Water	250 ml (8 fl oz / 1 cup)
Flax seeds	2 tsp, crushed
Walnuts	1 Tbsp, chopped
Soy milk	250 ml (8 fl oz / 1 cup)
Honey or black strap molasses	to taste

Method

1 Combine oats, bran meal and water in a saucepan. Bring to the boil over medium heat and stir to mix well. Reduce heat and leave to simmer for 3–5 minutes.

2 Add flax seeds, walnuts and milk. Leave to simmer for another 3–5 minutes and stir occasionally to prevent burning. Add honey or molasses to taste. Stir to mix well.

3 Dish out and serve immediately.

Post-Natal Care: Nature's Powers

The period between 40 and 60 days after giving birth is considered to be the most important recuperative period in the mother's life. According to Chinese healing philosophies, the quality of care and nutrition, or lack of it, will determine a woman's state of health for the rest of her life.

After the remarkable process and dramatic changes the body goes through in nurturing a new life and delivering it, the body will undergo something of an overhaul as it seeks to regenerate and replenish itself. At this point, the healing and recuperative power of the body is at its peak! It is said that if a woman has any chronic ailment, proper care during this period will heal the body of its health issues. That is the power of nature.

Post-natal Tips

A confinement lady with more than 20 years of experience in providing post-natal care shared these tips with me:

1. An immediate concern of many women is getting back into shape after giving birth. Instead of drinking plain water which might lead to bloating and edema, drink unpolished rice water (see below) to quench thirst.
2. While pig liver is good for replenishing blood and is an excellent confinement food, it should not be consumed too soon after giving birth, as it may cause skin freckles or pigmentation.

Unpolished Rice Water

An experienced confinement lady once told me that drinking plain water during the confinement period is a no-no. This is because it is too yin and may lead to bloatedness and water retention. She recommended drinking unpolished rice water as an alternative to plain water. *Serves 4–5*

Red unpolished rice	125 g (4^1/$_2$ oz)
Water	1.5 litres (48 fl oz / 6 cups)

Method

1. Wash and rinse rice 2–3 times, then spread out on a flat tray. Leave aside for 1–2 hours or until grains are completely dry.
2. Heat a frying pan over medium heat. Dry-fry rice for 15–20 minutes, stirring continuously to prevent burning. Meanwhile, bring water to the boil.
3. Remove rice from heat and transfer to a heatproof container. Once water has reached boling point, remove from heat and pour over rice immediately. Cover and leave mixture to infuse for 40 minutes. Water should be light reddish brown in colour.
4. Strain mixture and discard rice. Serve warm.

Slimming and Nourishing Soup

One of the main concerns of women after giving birth is to regain their pre-pregnancy figure. Slimming seems to contradict the principles of post-partum nutrition but losing weight doesn't mean starving one's body of nutrients. With proper nutrition, weight-loss can be achieved safely and effectively. This recipe stimulates metabolism and warms and enlivens various channels in the body and does not compromise on the supply of healing nutrients required by a woman during post-partum recovery. *Serves 3–4*

Garlic	6 cloves, peeled
Ginger	2.5-cm (1-in) knob, peeled and chopped
Black peppercorns	1 tsp
Celery seeds	$^1/_2$ tsp
Bay leaves	2
Lean beef	600 g (1 lb 5$^1/_3$ oz), sliced
Cooking oil	1 tsp
Onion	1, large, peeled and thinly sliced
Water	1.5 litres (48 fl oz / 6 cups)
Salt	to taste

Method

1 Combine garlic, ginger, peppercorns, celery seeds and bay leaves in a mortar. Using a pestle, pound until lightly crushed and fragrant. Set aside.

2 Bring a large pot of water to the boil and scald beef for about 20 seconds. Remove, dran and set aside.

3 Heat oil in a wok over medium heat and add beef and onion. Stir-fry for 3–5 minutes, or until fragrant. Beef should not be thoroughly cooked but lightly seared. Remove from heat and transfer to an earthen pot.

4 Add water and bring mixture to the boil over high heat. Skim off any fat or scum that rises to the surface. Reduce heat, add crushed ingredients and leave to simmer for 2 hours. Add salt to taste. Stir to mix well.

5 Dish out and serve immediately.

Sheng Hua Tang

Literally meaning "growth and dispel", *Sheng Hua Tang* is a classic confinement brew
that is de rigueur after giving birth. After giving birth, many women experience lower
abdominal pains, slow recovery of the uterus and vaginal area and anemia. Problems
like an incomplete discharge of the placenta and blood clots are also common. Only by
thoroughly eliminating the remnants of birth can there be full and smooth recovery of
the body and its reproductive organs. *Sheng Hua Tang* should be taken just once, 2–3 days
after delivery. I have advised that the tea be divided into two portions for consuming
once in the morning and once at night, so that the body can absorb it gradually.

Sheng Hua Tang Variation 1

Serves 1

Chinese angelica (*dang gui*)	4 *qian*	Prepared licorice (*zhi gan cao*)	$^1/_2$ *qian*
Prepared rehmannia (*shu di*)	2$^1/_2$ *qian*	Quick-fried ginger (*pao jiang*)	$^1/_2$ *qian*
Peach kernels (*tao ren*)	2$^1/_2$ *qian*, crushed	Water	500 ml (16 fl oz / 2 cups)
Ligusticum (*chuang xiong*)	2 *qian*		

Method

1 Rinse herbs and drain well. Place in an earthen pot, add 250 ml (8 fl oz / 1 cup) water and
leave to soak for 40 minutes.

2 Bring mixture to the boil over high heat, then reduce heat to low and leave to simmer for
40 minutes. Remove from heat and strain mixture into a large bowl. Return herbs to the
pot and set strained liquid aside.

3 Add remaining water to herbs and return to the boil over high heat. Reduce heat to low
and leave to simmer for 40 minutes, then remove from heat. Strain mixture into the same
bowl containing earlier strained liquid and discard herbs. Stir to mix well and divide into
2 portions.

4 Serve warm.

Sheng Hua Tang Variation 2

For women experiencing severe cramping and slow recovery of the cervix, add $^1/_2$ *qian*
Carthami Flos (*hong hua*) to *Sheng Hua Tang* Variation 1.

Sheng Hua Tang Variation 3

For symptoms like incomplete discharge of placenta resulting in cramps and bleeding,
omit prepared licorice (*zhi gan cao*) from the formula, replace fried ginger with fresh
ginger and add 3 *qian* motherwort (*yi mu cao*) and $^1/_2$ *qian* Carthami Flos (*hong hua*).

Motherwort Decoction

Blood stagnation after birth can result in abdominal pain and uterine bleeding. Motherwort is one of the most important herbs for relieving blood stagnation as it actively promotes circulation. At the same time, it stimulates the uterus, helping to dispel any residual placenta. It is also cooling and helps to purge toxins from the body. *Makes 2 portions*

Motherwort (*yi mu cao*)	3 *qian*
Water	500 ml (16 fl oz / 2 cups)

Method

1 Rinse motherwort and drain well. Place in an earthen pot, add 250 ml (8 fl oz / 1 cup) water and leave to soak for 30 minutes.

2 Bring mixture to the boil over high heat, then reduce heat to low and leave to simmer for 30 minutes. Remove from heat and strain mixture into a large bowl. Return motherwort to the pot and set strained liquid aside.

3 Add remaining water to herbs and return to the boil over high heat. Reduce heat to low and simmer for 30 minutes, then remove from heat. Strain mixture into the same bowl containing earlier strained liquid and discard motherwort. Stir to mix well and divide into 2 portions.

4 Serve warm.

Note: Not to be taken by those with blood deficiency or cold body constitutions. Avoid during pregnancy as motherwort has uterine stimulating properties. If reheating, do not allow tea to boil.

Lactation Tea

This tea features fennel seeds and fenugreek seeds, herbs which are traditionally used for promoting production of breast milk in lactating women. *Serves 1*

Fennel seeds	1 tsp
Fenugreek seeds	$1/2$ tsp
Freshly boiled water	250 ml (8 fl oz / 1 cup)
Honey (optional)	to taste

Method

1 Using a mortar and pestle, lightly crush fennel seeds and fenugreek seeds and place in a cup. Add water, cover and leave to infuse for 20 minutes.
2 Strain tea and add honey if desired. Serve warm.

Post-Lactation Tea

This tea can help relax and calm the mind. For women who wish to stop breastfeeding, this tea will help in ceasing the flow of breast milk. Menopausal women will also benefit from this tea as it can help balance the hormones and relieve hot flushes.

Dried sage	2 tsp
Freshly boiled water	250 ml (8 fl oz / 1 cup)
Honey	to taste

Method

1 Place sage in a cup and pour in water. Cover and leave to infuse for 30 minutes.
2 Strain tea and add honey to taste. Serve immediately.

Note: Not to be taken during pregnancy.

Minced Beef Porridge

A steaming bowl of porridge provides an easily digestable, yet nutritious meal when one does not have an appetite. *Serves 1*

Lean beef mince	200 g (7 oz)
Jasmine rice	55 g (2 oz) washed
Water	250 ml (8 fl oz / 1 cup)
Egg	1, beaten

Marinade

Light soy sauce	1 tsp
Dark soy sauce	1 tsp
Ground white pepper	$^1/_2$ tsp
Chinese rice wine or cooking sherry	$^1/_2$ tsp
Chopped ginger	$^1/_2$ tsp

Method

1 Prepare marinade. Combine ingredients in a mixing bowl and mix well. Add beef mince and use a spoon to mix evenly with marinade. Cover, refrigerate and leave to marinate for 1 hour.

2 Combine rice and water in a pot and bring to the boil. Reduce heat to low and add beef. Use a spatula to break meat up, then cover and leave to simmer for $1^1/_2$ hours. Stir occasionally to prevent burning.

3 Stir egg into porridge and mix well before serving, making sure egg is thoroughly cooked.

4 Dish out and serve immediately.

The Golden Years

I believe there is no exact age that marks the beginning of one's golden years. Rather, it comes gradually and hopefully, gracefully.

With proper nutrition and the right attitude, the golden years can be one of the best times yet in a person's life. Getting older is a natural progression of life. It is perfectly fine to spot some wrinkles or silver hair, walk a bit slower, and look a bit older. What really matters is that one continues to possess good health, a strong, clear mind and the capacity to live life to its fullest. The recipes in this chapter provide excellent nutrition support for the golden years.

Make sure that your intake of calcium is adequate. Calcium can be found in foods like milk, cheese, yoghurt, molasses, fish, tofu, sesame seeds and seaweed. If you are lactose intolerant, avoid cow's milk and drink goat's milk instead. To ensure optimal absorption of calcium, make sure you consume Vitamin D (by getting a bit of sunlight before 11am every day) and Vitamin K (found in vegetables like spinach, cabbage and cauliflower).

- Minimise your intake of soft drinks, salt, fats, caffeine and sugar.

- Avoid smoking.

- Eat your daily servings of fruit and vegetables. They are rich in antioxidants and other vitamins and minerals that keep your body cells functioning healthily.

- Drink homemade herbal soups regularly. Soups have lots of nutrients and are easily absorbed by the body.

- If you experience weak legs or knees, change your daily staple of white rice to unpolished rice.

- A small amount of red wine or herbal wine each day (about 30–50 ml) helps to promote circulation and enhance your body's metabolism. Don't drink alcohol excessively.

- Eat adequately but not excessively. Don't overload on proteins and red meats.

- Do light exercises regularly. Go for walks in the park, or practise tai chi by the beach for instance. Enjoy your exercise!

Miso Soup (*recipe page 122*)

Herbal Porridge

The lotus seeds give this dish an added crunch and sweetness, while strengthening the spleen and kidneys. *Serves 1*

Chinese yam (*shan yao*)	1 *qian*
Chinese angelica (*dang gui*)	1 *qian*
Chinese wolfberries (*gou qi zi*)	1 *qian*
Lotus seeds (*lian zi*)	6 pieces, seeded
Brown (unpolished) rice	55 g (2 oz), washed and drained
Water	625 ml (20 fl oz / 2^1/$_2$ cups)
Salt	to taste

Method

1 Rinse herbs and drain well. Break Chinese yam and angelica into small pieces, then place in an earthen pot.
2 Add remaining herbs, rice and water and bring to the boil over high heat. Reduce heat to medium-low, cover and leave to cook for 2 hours, stirring occasionally to prevent sticking. Add more water, if necessary. Add salt to taste.
3 Dish out and serve immediately.

Note: Avoid consumption during pregnancy.

Black Jujube Tea

Black jujube has a pleasantly sweet, slightly smoky flavour. It is an excellent anti-aging tonic as it not only nourishes the blood and energy, but keeps the mind calm and relaxed. A combination of these two factors will keep you looking and feeling young. *Makes 4–5 portions*

Black jujube *(nan zao)*	10 pieces, crushed
Water	1.25 litres (40 fl oz / 5 cups)

Method

1 Place jujube and water in an earthen pot and bring to the boil over high heat, then reduce heat to low and leave to simmer for 30 minutes.
2 Remove pot from heat and leave aside to further infuse for 10 minutes. Strain and discard jujubes.
3 Serve warm.

Note: Avoid consumption if you have flu with thick, hot phlegm, or are experiencing excess body heat or dampness.

Miso Soup

This is a simple but highly nutritious and satisfying dish. *Serves 1*

Dried wakame seaweed	1 tsp, rinsed and drained
Water	500 ml (16 fl oz / 2 cups)
Small carrot	1, peeled and cubed
Silken tofu	45 g ($1^1/_2$ oz), cubed
Miso paste	1 Tbsp

Method

1 Place wakame in a small earthen pot. Add water and leave to soak until wakame has softened.

2 Add carrot to pot and bring mixture to the boil over high heat. Reduce heat to medium-low, cover and leave to simmer for $1^1/_2$ hours. Add more water, if necessary. Add tofu in the last 10 minutes of cooking. Remove from heat and stir in miso paste.

3 Dish out and serve immediately, with plain rice.

Tip: When buying miso, choose those that do not contain MSG.

Nature's Tidbits

Miso

Miso is rich in proteins, vitamins and minerals which are essential for keeping the body healthy and youthful. As a soy product, it is a good source of isoflavone, which helps prevent breast cancer and heart diseases.

Fish Maw Soup

This delicious soup has great anti-aging properties. *Serves 4–5*

Dried scallops	85 g (3 oz)
Astragalus (*huang qi*)	3 *qian*
Red dates (*hong zao*)	8
Chinese wolfberries (*gou qi zi*)	1 Tbsp
Chicken	1, cleaned, skinned and chopped
Coarse salt	2–3 Tbsp
Water	2.5 litres (80 fl oz / 10 cups)
Dried fish maw	125 g (4$\frac{1}{2}$ oz), soaked in hot water to soften and cut into bite-size pieces
Salt	to taste

Method

1 Combine scallops and herbs in a bowl and add enough water to cover herbs. Leave to soak for 40 minutes.

2 Meanwhile, rub chicken with thoroughly with salt and place in a large earthen pot. Add water and bring to the boil over high heat. Skim off any fat or scum that rises to the surface, then add fish maw and herb and scallop mixture and return to the boil. Reduce heat to low, cover and leave to simmer for 2 hours. Add salt to taste and stir to mix well.

3 Dish out and serve immediately.

Note: Omit astragalus from the recipe if you wish to consume this during pregnancy.

Nature's Tidbits

Fish maw
Fish maw is virtually tasteless, although it may be a little fishy. It is rich in collagen and elastin, which helps to keep the skin firm and smooth, and ligaments healthy and supple.

Tea recipes for relieving hot flushes

There are many hypotheses as to what causes hot flushes during menopause. In traditional Chinese medicine, hot flushes are said to be due to heat in the blood and a *yin* deficiency. According to Western medical theory, hot flushes are caused by major hormonal changes which in turn, cause the blood vessels to dilate. The following two recipes are useful for alleviating hot flushes. For best results, drink twice daily until symptoms abate.

Hot Flushes and Mood Swings Relief Tea

Serves 1

Glossy privet fruit (*nu zhen zi*)	2 *qian*
Eclipta(*han lian cao*)	2 *qian*
Stellaria root (*yin chai hu*)	2 *qian*
Albizia flowers (*he huan hua*)	2 *qian*
Oyster shell (*mu li*)	2 *qian*
Water	500 ml (16 fl oz / 2 cups)

Method

1 Rinse herbs and drain well. Using a mortar and pestle, crush privet fruit lightly and place in a bowl. Add eclipta, stellaria root and albizia flowers and 250 ml (8 fl oz / 1 cup) water. Leave mixture to soak for 40 minutes.

2 Place oyster shell in an earthen pot and add 125 ml (4 fl oz / $^1/_2$ cup) water. Bring to the boil over high heat for 10 minutes, then add herbal mixture and return to the boil. Reduce heat to low and leave to simmer for 30 minutes.

3 Remove from heat and strain mixture into a large bowl. Return herbs to the pot and set strained liquid aside.

4 Add remaining water to herbs and return to the boil over high heat. Reduce heat to low and simmer for 30 minutes, then remove from heat. Strain mixture into the same bowl containing earlier strained liquid and discard herbs. Stir to mix well and divide into 2 portions.

5 Serve warm.

Nature's Tidbits

Glossy privet fruit (*nu zhen zi*)
Glossy privet fruit is nourishes *yin* and dispels excess heat. It also helps reduce irritability and mood swings.

Elipta (*han lian cao*)
Elipta nourishes *yin* and reduces heat in the blood vessels, preventing the vessels from becoming overly dilated.

Stellaria root (*yin chai hu*)
Stellaria root is considered to be a mild and cooling herb. It is often used to relieve irritability, heat, night sweats and excess body heat.

Albizia flowers (*he huan hua*)
Albizia flowers help calm the mind and spirit, stabilise the emotions and improve sleep.

Hot Flushes Relief Tea

Serves 1

Peony bark (*mu dan pi*)	2 *qian*
Fresh rehmannia (*sheng di*)	2 *qian*
Anemarrhena (*zhi mu*)	2 *qian*
Water	500 ml (16 fl oz / 2 cups)

Method

1 Rinse herbs and drain well. Place in an earthen pot, add water and leave mixture to soak for 40 minutes.

2 Bring mixture to the boil over high heat, then reduce heat to low and leave to simmer for 40 minutes. Remove from heat and strain mixture. Discard herbs and divide into 2 portions.

3 Serve warm.

Note: Avoid consumption if experiencing symptoms of cold, diarrhea, or weakness in the stomach and spleen.

Nature's Tidbits

Peony bark (*mu dan pi*)
Peony bark helps to regulate blood circulation and dispel blood stagnation. It also cools blood and dispels excess heat.

Fresh rehmannia (*sheng di*)
In this formula, fresh rehmannia is used for its blood cooling and heat-dispelling properties. During menopause, women frequently experience *yin* deficiency. Fresh rehmannia addresses this problem by nourishing the *yin* at the same time.

Anemarrhena (*zhi mu*)
Anemarrhena is frequently used for relieving menopausal symptoms such as hot flushes and irritability, as it nourishes the *yin* and dispels heat.

Elixir of Youth for Women

This is an excellent tonic for general health and beauty, particularly for women aged 21 and above. Take 30 ml (1 fl oz / 1 Tbsp) twice daily, once before dinner on an empty stomach and once before bedtime. In cold weather, you may like to increase the dosage slightly. *Makes about 1.5 litres (48 fl oz / 6 cups)*

Chinese angelica (*dang gui*)	3 *qian*
White peony bark (*bai shao*)	3 *qian*
Ligusticum (*chuan xiong*)	3 *qian*
Codonopsis root (*dang shen*)	3 *qian*
Chinese wolfberries (*gou qi zi*)	3 *qian*
Chinese yam (*shan yao*)	3 *qian*
Cistanche (*rou cong rong*)	3 *qian*
Black jujube (*nan zao*)	2 *qian*
Licorice (*gan cao*)	1 *qian*
Liquor such as rice wine or vodka (80%-proof)	1.5 litres (48 fl oz / 6 cups)
Honey (optional)	to taste

Method

1 Rinse herbs and drain well. Blot dry with paper towels. Arrange on a large tray and leave aside to dry completely in a clean, dry and airy place for 2–3 days.

2 Transfer herbs to a large glass jar. Pour in 1 litre (32 fl oz / 4 cups) liquor, making sure herbs are completely immersed. Seal jar tightly and store in a cool, dry and dark place for 3 months. Shake the glass jar once a week to encourage the extraction process.

3 Strain half of herb and liquor mixture into a glass bottle and seal tightly. Add remaining liquor and reseal jar. Return to storage for another 3 months.

4 Strain herb and liquor mixture into glass bottle containing the first strain. Shake bottle to mix well and add honey to taste, if desired. Store in a cool, dark place.

Note: Not to be taken during menstruation, pregnancy or lactation.

Longevity Tea

The herbs in this tea work synergistically to strengthen the body, enhance the immune functions, fortify the heart and improve the physical and mental sense of well being. *Serves 2*

Garnoderma (*ling zhi*)	4 *qian*
Brown (unpolished) rice	1 Tbsp
Gynostemma (*jiao gu lan*)	2 *qian*
Astragalus (*huang qi*)	3 *qian*
Water	625 ml (20 fl oz / 2^1/$_2$ cups)

Method

1 Rinse herbs and drain well. Place ganoderma in an earthen pot, add 300 ml (10 fl oz / 1^1/$_4$ cups) water and leave to soak for 30 minutes. Bring to the boil over high heat, then reduce heat to low, cover and leave to simmer for 1^1/$_2$ hours.

2 Meanwhile, place gynostemma, astragalus and unpolished rice in a bowl. Add remaining water and leave to soak for 30 minutes., then add to garnoderma in pot and return to the boil. Reduce heat to low and leave to simmer for 25 minutes. Strain mixture and discard rice and herbs.

3 Serve warm.

Note: This tea may have a slightly sedative effect, and is thus best drunk before bedtime. Do not consume during pregnancy and on an empty stomach.

Nature's Tidbits

Garnoderma (*ling zhi*)

Garnoderma is well known for its immune enhancing and regulating functions. In addition, it helps to reduce cholesterol and excess fatty deposits. Hence, it is useful for improving cardiovascular health. Garnoderma is also rich in antioxidants which are essential for protecting the body's cells from free radical damage.

Gynostemma (*jiao gu lan*)

Gynostemma strengthens the body by helping it to cope with stress and change. It improves one's energy level and mental clarity, and is considered to be an excellent anti-aging herb.

Astragalus (*huang qi*)

Astragalus promotes the production of *qi* and blood while enhancing the body's immune system.

For Men Only

The modern man of today is under pressure to be financially stable and maintain a career. He is also expected to be romantic, sensitive, intellectually stimulating, have a good sense of humour and be willing to help out with the children and domestic chores. It would also be a bonus if he could cook.

To cope and thrive amid such expectations, a man has to be in tip-top condition, both physically and mentally. While blood is the key to a woman's health, a man's vitality is closely associated with his kidneys. So when it comes to addressing specific health concerns related to men, some of which include premature ejaculation, impotence or balding, the kidneys, which is the centre of his life-force energy are often the focal point of attention.

Of course, the kidneys are in turn affected by the health of other parts of the body through an intricate interplay of energies among the organs. But that is another story which would extend beyond the scope of this book.

For now, I will focus on recipes that nourish and energise the kidneys. To supplement the recipes here, refer to Chapter 6, *Nourishment For Fabulous Hair*.

Vegetable Juice for a Healthy Prostrate (*recipe page 130*)

Prostate Health

The prostate gland is a key area of concern for men as surveys indicate that a growing number of men over the age of 50 experience prostate problems. Follow these guidelines to maintain good prostate health.

Do:

- Drink plenty of water every day to flush out toxins and bacteria from your bladder and kidneys. Visit the washroom if you must. Do not hold back or control urination for prolonged periods.

- Consume plenty of fresh, whole foods and fruit rich in natural nutrients and fibre. Eat foods with high-quality proteins from fish, soy products, yoghurt and lean meat. In place of peanuts, eat pumpkin seeds, sunflower seeds and walnuts.

- Consume alcohol in moderation. A bit of red wine (one glass a day) is good as it supplies your body with antioxidants that enhance cardiovascular health and helps to promote overall circulation.

- Keep your weight and BMI within the normal range for your height.

- Take herbal supplements such as Saw Palmetto, which is lauded for keeping the prostrate gland healthy. Pomegranate juice also has the same beneficial effects.

Don't:

- Don't consume too much cured meats such as bacon, sausages and ham. As delicious as they are, their high salt content will cause long-term damage to the kidneys and cause balding.

- Don't consume saturated fats such lard, ghee and other animal fats.

Vegetable Juice for a Healthy Prostate

Drinking this concoction regularly will help to keep the prostate healthy as it is rich in natural antioxidants, beta carotene and lycopene, which help reduce the risk of prostate cancer. Steaming the tomatoes will help to enable the lycopene to be easily absorbed by the body. Garlic enhances the antibacterial and cholesterol-lowering properties of this concoction, which go a long way in keeping the prostate gland in tip-top condition. *Serves 1*

Tomatoes	2
Extra virgin olive oil	2 Tbsp
Carrots	3, small, peeled and chopped
Beetroot	$^1/_2$, peeled and chopped
Garlic	1 clove, peeled and crushed

Method

1 Steam tomatoes over low-medium heat for 30 minutes, or until soft, with juices running. Cut into quarters and place in a bowl, then drizzle with olive oil, cover and set aside for 30 minutes.

2 Place tomatoes and remaining ingredients in a blender and blend until smooth.

3 Pour out and serve immediately.

Strengthening Stew

This delicious stew will fortify and nourish your body. *Serves 2*

Duck	1, 500 g (1 lb 1¹/₂ oz), cleaned and skinned
Coarse salt	2–3 Tbsp
Black soy sauce	180 ml (6 fl oz / ³/₄ cup)
Ground pepper	2 tsp
Eucommia bark (*du zhong*)	3 *qian*
Chinese wolfberries (*gou qi zi*)	1 Tbsp
Water	500 ml (16 fl oz / 2 cups)
Sea cucumber	3, soaked to soften and cut into 2.5-cm (1-in) pieces
Ginger	5-cm (2-in) knob, peeled and sliced
Spring onions (scallions)	2, finely sliced
Vegetable oil	2 Tbsp
Dried shiitake mushrooms	10, soaked to soften with stalks removed
Chinese rice wine	3 Tbsp

Method

1 Rub duck thoroughly with salt. Rinse and drain, then chop into small pieces. Place in a large bowl, add black soy sauce and ground pepper and leave aside to marinate for 1 hour.

2 Rinse eucommia bark and Chinese wolfberries and drain well. Place in a bowl, add water and leave to soak for 40 minutes.

3 Heat a non-stick wok over medium heat and dry-fry sea cucumber, ginger and spring onions for 5 minutes or until fragrant. Remove from heat and set aside.

4 Using the same wok, heat oil over high heat. Add duck and mushrooms and stir-fry for 5 minutes. Return sea cucumber, ginger and spring onions to the wok. Add herb mixture and bring to the boil. Reduce heat to low, cover and leave to simmer for 1 hour, or until duck is cooked and tender.

5 Dish out and serve immediately.

Nature's Tidbits

Sea cucumber

Sea cucumber is valued for its kidney strengthening and blood cleansing properties. It also helps to lower blood pressure. It is rich in chondroitin sulfate, which is essential for maintaining healthy, pain-free joints and strong connective tissues.

Eucommia bark (*du zhong*)

Eucommia bark helps to tone and strengthen the kidneys and liver, and is often used to treat kidney or liver-deficiency symptoms such as lower body pains, premature ejaculation and coldness and weakness in the joints or bones. It is also useful in lowering blood pressure as it helps to dilate blood vessels. It is therefore considered to be potentially useful in treating hypertension.

Ayurvedic Almond Milk

This warming and strengthening formula is reputed to replenish energy, and can also be considered as an aphrodisiac. *Serves 1*

Almonds	125 g (4^1/$_2$ oz), finely ground
Water	250 ml (8 fl oz / 1 cup)
Ground cardamom	a pinch
Ground cinnamon	a pinch
Ground cloves	a pinch
Saffron strands	6
Honey	to taste

Method

1 Combine almonds and water in a saucepan and bring to the boil over high heat. Reduce heat to low, then bring to a gentle simmer for 5–8 minutes, stirring constantly. Remove from heat and set aside to cool slightly.

2 Transfer mixture to a blender and blend until smooth. Using a muslin cloth, strain mixture into a saucepan to obtain the milk. Discard residue. Add cardamom, cinnamon, cloves and saffron strands and heat gently over medium heat. Leave mixture to simmer for 5 minutes without boiling.

3 Add honey to taste and stir to mix well. Serve warm.

Nature's Tidbits

Almonds
Packed with proteins, vitamins, minerals and nutritive oils, almond provides overall nourishment for the body. Almond milk is more easily digested by the body and is a great substitute for cow's milk, especially for those who are lactose intolerant.

Cardamom
Cardamom helps to improve digestion and is reputed to have good aphrodisiacal properties.

Cinnamon
Cinnamon is a warming herb that is used to tonify the kidney's *yang* energy. Due to its warming nature, it is efficient at dispelling cold in channels, or meridians, which are like pathways and points throughout the body where energy travels and flows, and the middle section of the body, thus helping to clear stagnation and blockages in the energy pathways. In addition, it helps in the production of *yang* energy and stimulates its movement throughout the entire body, thus encouraging blood production at the same time.

Cloves
Cloves are useful in eliminating bad odours in food and keeping one's breath fresh and sweet.

Saffron
Saffron is one of the most expensive spices in the world, and is reputed to be a top aphrodisiac for both men and women.

Tonifying Porridge

This simple porridge is an excellent source of nourishment for men. *Serves 1*

Red (unpolished) rice	55 g (2 oz)
Chinese yam (*shan yao*)	2 *qian*
Fox nuts (*qian shi*)	2 *qian*
Lotus seeds (*lian zi*)	2 *qian*, pitted and soaked in water for 3 hours
Water	750 ml (24 fl oz / 3 cups)
Salt (optional)	to taste

Method

1 Rinse all ingredients and drain well. Place in a small earthen pot, add water and bring to the boil over high heat. Reduce heat to low, cover and leave to cook for 2–3 hours, stirring occasionally to prevent sticking. Add more water if necessary.

2 Add salt to taste, if desired. Dish out and serve immediately.

Note: Omit lotus seeds if constipated.

Nature's Tidbits

Chinese yam (*shan yao*)
Chinese yam is a highly versatile herb. In this recipe, it is used for its ability to tonify and consolidate the kidneys' *yin* energy and essence due to its astringent nature.

Fox nuts (*qian shi*)
Fox nuts help to remove dampness, tonify the spleen and kidneys as well as consolidate the kidneys' essence.

Essence Nourishing Soup

This soup provides excellent nourishment for the body's vital essence and helps to dispel weakness, night sweating and insomnia. *Serves 3–4*

Dried oysters	250 g (9 oz)
Dried scallops	85 g (3 oz)
Lotus seeds (*lian zhi*)	45 g (1 1/2 oz)
Dried shiitake mushrooms	6, caps wiped and stalks removed
Water	2 litres (8 cups)
Salt	to taste

Method

1 Rinse all ingredients and drain well. Place in an earthen pot, add water and leave to soak for 1 hour. Bring to the boil over high heat, then reduce heat to low and leave to simmer for 2 hours. Add salt to taste and stir to mix well.

2 Dish out and serve immediately.

Robust Wine

This is a classic herbal wine formula specially created for men to boost libido and treat impotence. Take 2 Tbsp twice daily, once before dinner on an empty stomach and once before bedtime. In cold weather, you may like to increase the dosage slightly.

Makes about 1 litre (32 fl oz / 4 cups)

Epimedium (*yin yang huo*)	3 *qian*	Prepared rehmannia (*shu di*)	3 *qian*
Chinese wolfberries (*gou qi zi*)	3 *qian*	Wheat (*xiao mai*)	3 *qian*
Cistanche (*rou cong rong*)	3 *qian*	Cynomorium (*suo yang*)	3 *qian*
Cornus fruit (*shan zhu yu*)	3 *qian*	Liquor such as rice wine or vodka (80%-proof)	1.5 litre (48 fl oz / 6 cups)
Morinda root (*ba ji tian*)	3 *qian*		

Method

1 Rinse herbs and drain well. Blot dry with paper towels. Arrange on a large tray and leave aside to dry completely in a clean, dry and airy place for 2–3 days.

2 Place herbs in a large glass jar. Pour in 1 litre (32 fl oz / 4 cups) liquor, making sure herbs are completely immersed. Seal jar tightly and store in a cool, dry and dark place for 3 months. Shake the glass jar once a week to encourage the extraction process.

3 Strain half of herb and liquor mixture into a glass bottle and seal tightly. Add remaining liquor and reseal jar. Return to storage for another 3 months.

4 Strain herb and liquor mixture into glass bottle containing the first strain of herbal wine. Shake bottle to mix well and add honey to taste, if desired. Store in a cool, dark place.

Note: Men with a high libido or who experience premature ejaculation should not consume this wine. Avoid consumption if experiencing diarrhea, excess body heat and flu.

Nature's Tidbits

Cistanche (*rou cong rong*)
Cistanche is a useful herb for treating impotence in men and infertility in women as it replenishes the kidneys' *yang* and essence.

Cornus fruit (*shan zhu yu*)
Cornus fruit tonifies both the liver and kidneys, and prevents excessive loss of important body fluids.

Morinda root (*ba ji tian*)
Morinda root nourishes the kidneys' *yang*, helping to correct deficiency symptoms such as impotence, incontinence and spermatorrhea.

Wheat (*xiao mai*)
Wheat treats anxiety, irritability and depression, which can dampen a man's libido. It also nourishes the heart.

Cynomorium (*suo yang*)
Cynomorium works by tonifying the kidneys' *yang* and essence. In addition, it also tonifies the liver's *yin* and blood.

Vitality soup

Other than making this a delicious dish, the herbs used are particularly good for revitalising a tired body. *Serves 4–5*

Cordyceps (*dong chong xia cao*)	2 *qian*
Epimedium (*yin yang huo*)	2 *qian*
Prepared rehmannia (*shu di*)	1 *qian*
Chinese wolfberries (*gou qi zi*)	2 tsp
Dried orange peel (*chen pi*)	2 pieces
Duck	1, 1 kg (2 lb 3 oz), cleaned, excess fat trimmed
Coarse salt	2–3 Tbsp
Salt	to taste

Method

1 Rinse herbs and drain well. Place in a bowl, add enough water to cover herbs and leave to soak for 30 minutes.

2 Rub duck thoroughly with salt, then rinse. Chop into small pieces and place in an earthen pot. Add 2 litres (64 fl oz / 8 cups) water and bring to the boil over high heat. Skim off any fat or scum that rises to the surface. Add herb mixture and return to the boil, then reduce heat to low, cover and leave to simmer for 2 hours. Add salt to taste and stir to mix well.

3 Dish out and serve immediately.

Nature's Tidbits

Cordyceps (*dong chong xia cao*)

Cordyceps is a very important herb for treating deficiencies of the kidney's *yang* energy and fluids. Such conditions include impotence, premature ejaculation, spermatorrhea and lower back and knee pain.

Epimedium (*yin yang hua*)

Epimedium tonifies the kidney's *yang* energy and enhances libido. It is often used to treat conditions such as lack of sexual desire, soft erection, premature ejaculation and low sperm count. In addition, it removes blockages in the body's energy channels caused by coldness, wind and dampness, thus relieving pain and numbness in the limbs, tendons and muscles.

Lower Back Strengthening Soup

This soup is a great source of nourishment for those who experience pain and weakness in the lower back, knees and legs. *Serves 2–3*

Black beans	45 g (1^1/$_2$ oz)
Eucommia bark (*du zhong*)	3 *qian*
Chinese wolfberries (*gou qi zi*)	3 *qian*
Cnidium (*chuan xiong*)	3 *qian*
Cyathula root (*chuan niu xi*)	3 *qian*
Pig's tail	300 g (10^1/$_2$ oz), cleaned, excess fat trimmed and chopped
Salt (optional)	to taste

Method

1 Place black beans and herbs in a bowl of water to soak for 1 hour.

2 Bring a pot of water to the boil and scald pig's tail twice for about 20 seconds each time. Remove, drain and place in an earthen pot.

3 Add 1.5 litres (48 fl oz / 6 cups) water and bring to the boil over high heat. Skim off any fat or scum that rises to the surface. Add black bean and herb mixture and return mixture to the boil, then reduce heat to low and leave to simmer for 3 hours, or until pig's tail is tender. Add salt to taste, if desired.

4 Dish out and serve immediately.

Nature's Tidbits

Cyathula root (*chuan niu xi / niu xi*)

Cyathula root promotes blood circulation and dispels blood stasis. It is often used to relieve musculoskeletal pain due to sports injuries. Cyathula root is also relieves lower back pain, sore knees, swelling caused by excess body heat and dampness.

Chinese Herbs To Avoid During Pregnancy

There are many Chinese herbs should not be consumed during pregnancy as they may endanger the fetus. Some herbs cause the uterine to contract, thus increasing chances of a miscarriage. I have compiled the following list of herbs that one should avoid, to the best of my knowledge. It is not, however, an exhaustive list, so do consult a qualified Chinese physician when in doubt, or before using herbs that are not stated in this list.

- Achyranthes root (*huai niu xi*)
- Aconite (*fu zi*)
- Aconite tsaowu (*cao wu*)
- Albizia bark (*he huan pi*)
- Aloe vera (*lu hui*)
- Arisaema (*tian nan xing*)
- Arisaema pulvis (*dan nan xing*)
- Aristolochia herb (*tian xian teng*)
- Aromatic turmeric tuber (*yu jin*)
- Artemisiae anomalae (*liu ji nu*)
- Astragalus (*huang qi*)
- Bamboo leaves (*zhu ye*)
- Basil (*jiu ceng ta*)
- Belamcanda (*she gan*)
- Betel nut (*bing lang*)
- Betel nut Peel (*da fu pi*)
- Bezoar (*niu huang*)
- Bitter orange (*zhi ke*)
- Borneol (*bing pian*)
- Brucea seed (*ya dan zi*)
- Calomel (*qing fen*)
- Camphor (*zhang nao*)
- Cassia seeds (*jue ming zi*)
- Cattail pollen (*pu huang*)
- Centipede (*wu gong*)
- Chinese wolfberry (*gou qi zi*)
- Cinnamon bark (*rou gui*)
- Cinnamon twigs (*gui zhi*)
- Citron fruit (*xiang yuan*)
- Coix seeds (*yi yi ren*)
- Common andrographis herb (*chuan xin lian*)
- Common club moss (*shen jin cao*)
- Common lophatherum (*dan zhu ye*)
- Corydalis (*yan hu suo*)
- Crotin fruit (*ba dou*)
- Curcuma zedoaria (*e zhu*)
- Cyathula root (*chuan niu xi /niu xi*)
- Descurainia (*ting li zi*)
- Dianthus (*qu mai*)
- Dragon's blood (*xue jie*)
- Dried ginger (*gan jiang*)
- Dried lacquer (*gan qi*)
- Dryopteris root (*guan zhong*)
- Earthworm (*di long*)
- Ephedra (*ma huang*)
- Euphorbia (*da ji*)
- Eupolyphaga (*di bie chong*)
- Fennel seed (*xiao hui xiang*)
- Fenugreek seed (*hu lu ba*)
- Frankincense (*ru xiang*)
- Gadfly (*meng chong*)
- Genkwa flower (*yuan hua*)
- Gan sui root (*gan sui*)
- Gingko nut (*bai guo*)
- Gleditsia Fruit (*zao jiao*)
- Gleditsia Spine (*zao jiao ci*)
- Gotu kola (*ji xue cao*)
- Halloysite (*chi shi zhi*)
- Hematite (*dai zhe shi*)
- Hydnocarpus seed (*da feng zi*)
- Immature bitter or sweet orange (*zhi shi*)
- Indian stringbush (*pu yin*)
- Japanese thistle (*da ji*)
- Kalopanacis (*niao bu su*)
- Leech (*shui zhi*)
- Leucas (*hu yao huang*)
- Liquidambar (*lu lu tong*)
- Lindernia (*ding jing cao*)
- Litharge (*mi tuo seng*)
- Magnolia bark (*hou pu*)
- Malva (*dong kui zi*)
- Massa fermentata (*shen qu*)
- Minium (*qian dan*)
- Mirabilis (*zhu hua fan tou*)
- Momordica seeds (*mu bie zi*)
- Motherwort herb (*yi mu cao*)
- Musk (*she xiang*)
- Mylabris (*ban mao*)
- Myrhh (*mo yao*)
- Notoginseng (*san qi*)
- Ophicalcite (*hua rui shi*)
- Paris rhizome (*zao xiu*)
- Peach kernel (*tao ren*)
- Pepper (*hu jiao*)
- Pharbitis seed (*qian niu zi*)
- Physalis angulata (*pao zai cao*)
- Poke root (*shang lu*)
- Polygonum cuspidatum (*hu zhang*)
- Psoralea fruit (*bu gu zi*)
- Rhinoceros horn (*xi jiao*)
- Rhubarb root (*da huang*)
- Rough horsetail (*mu zei*)
- Safflower (*hong hua*)
- Sandalwood (*tan xiang*)
- Sappan wood (*su mu*)
- Schefflera (*qi ye lian*)
- Scorpion (*quan xie*)
- Scutellaria (*huang qin*)
- Seahorse (*hai ma*)
- Semen strychni (*ma qian zi*)
- Senna leaves (*fan xie ye*)
- Siberian milkwort root (*yuan zhi*)
- Sichuan aconite (*chuan wu*)
- Siegesbeckia (*xi xian cao*)
- Sodium sulfate (*mang xiao*)
- Sparganium (*san ling*)
- Spatholobus (*ji xue teng*)
- Spiny date seed (*suan zao ren*)
- Stellaria (*cha chi huang*)
- Sulfur (*liu huang*)
- Xanthium fruit (*cang er zi*)
- Tetrapanax (*tong cao*)
- Toad venum (*chan su*)
- Torreya seeds (*fei zi*)
- Tortoise plastron (*gui ban*)
- Tree peony bark (*mu dan pi*)
- Tribulus (*bai ji li*)
- Trichosanthes root (*tian hua fen*)
- Tripterygium (*lei gong teng*)
- Trogopterus dung (*wu ling zhi*)
- Turmeric (*huang jiang*)
- Turtle shell (*bie jia*)
- Typhonium (*bai fu zi*)
- Vaccaria seeds (*wang bu liu xing*)
- Veratrum root and Rhizome (*li lu*)
- Verbena (*ma bian cao*)
- Zanthoxylum (*hua jiao*)

Glossary of Herbs

Achyranthes root
牛膝

Adenophora
南沙参

Astragalus
黄芪

Biota seeds
柏子仁

Black jujube
南枣

Cassia seed
决明子

Chinese angelica
当归

Chinese yam
山药

Coix seeds
薏苡仁

Cnidium
川芎

Cyperus
香附

Dahurican
angelica root
白芷

Dandelion
蒲公英

Eclipta
旱莲草

Eucommia bark
杜仲

Fleece
flower root
何首乌

Garnoderma
灵芝

Glossy privet fruit
女贞子

Hawthorne fruit
山楂

Honeysuckle
金银花

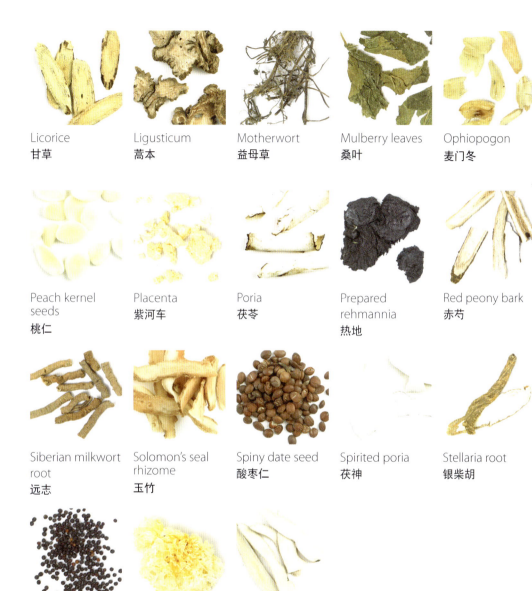

Licorice
甘草

Ligusticum
藁本

Motherwort
益母草

Mulberry leaves
桑叶

Ophiopogon
麦门冬

Peach kernel
seeds
桃仁

Placenta
紫河车

Poria
茯苓

Prepared
rehmannia
热地

Red peony bark
赤芍

Siberian milkwort
root
远志

Solomon's seal
rhizome
玉竹

Spiny date seed
酸枣仁

Spirited poria
茯神

Stellaria root
银柴胡

Vaccaria seeds
王不留行

White fungus
白木耳

White peony bark
白芍